Power at Play

Also by Niels Åkerstrøm Andersen

PARTNERSHIPS: MACHINES OF POSSIBILITY

DISCURSIVE ANALYTICAL STRATEGIES: Understanding Foucault, Koselleck, Laclau, Luhmann

Power at Play

The Relationships between Play, Work and Governance

Niels Åkerstrøm Andersen
Professor in Public and Political Management, Department of Management Politics and Philosophy, Copenhagen Business School (CBS)

First published 2009 by
PALGRAVE MACMILLAN

Palgrave Macmillan in the UK is an imprint of Macmillan Publishers Limited,
registered in England, company number 785998, of Houndmills, Basingstoke,
Hampshire RG21 6XS.

Palgrave Macmillan in the US is a division of St Martin's Press LLC,
175 Fifth Avenue, New York, NY 10010.

Palgrave Macmillan is the global academic imprint of the above companies
and has companies and representatives throughout the world.

Palgrave® and Macmillan® are registered trademarks in the United States,
the United Kingdom, Europe and other countries.

ISBN: 978–0–230–22820–7

This book is printed on paper suitable for recycling and made from fully
managed and sustained forest sources. Logging, pulping and manufacturing
processes are expected to conform to the environmental regulations of the
country of origin.

A catalogue record for this book is available from the British Library.

A catalog record for this book is available from the Library of Congress.

10   9   8   7   6   5   4   3   2   1
18   17   16   15   14   13   12   11   10   09

Printed and bound in Great Britain by
CPI Antony Rowe, Chippenham and Eastbourne

Contents

List of Figures and Tables

Figures

Tables

Acknowledgements

This book began as a collaborative work for an article with Hanne Knudsen, and a number of the basic ideas in this book have been developed together with her. Hanne Knudsen is currently writing her PhD dissertation at the Danish School of Education (DPU) about the cross field of school management and home–school cooperation. When it became clear that the article was to expand into a book, I continued the project on my own while she devoted her time to her dissertation. In the last part of the book I discuss a number of games played within a school environment. These are taken from Hanne's dissertation work and could not have been written without her collaboration. Therefore, I would like to express my gratitude to her.

In addition, I would like to thank Christina Thyssen who has translated the book into English. Also thanks to Gorm Madsen, Joakim Kromann Rasmussen and Helene Ratner who have assisted me generally and in obtaining the material for the book. Thanks to Liv Bjerge, my contact at the Copenhagen Business School Library. She has been an invaluable help. I would also like to thank my colleagues for many good discussions and a number of course participants, students, and others with whom I have discussed this project and who were often able to share examples and contexts that I had not been aware of. My thanks also extend to the Velux Foundation who supported our large project Management of Self-Management at the Department of Management, Politics and Philosophy, Copenhagen Business School.

Finally, I would like to thank Asmund Born, who is the best reader I know. Like so many times before, he has provided me with critical and inspiring arguments and compelled me to do my best.

This book has proven a rather enjoyable project because it has led to travels into both empirical and theoretical corners, of which I was not aware, and as the project progressed an increasing number of doors have opened. Although my understanding of play and organization has clearly increased significantly with this work I believe that I have only started to scratch the surface of this field, which calls for future studies.

NIELS ÅKERSTRØM ANDERSEN

Introduction

The statistics of trade and production could not fail to introduce a sporting element into economic life. In consequence,
there is now a sporting side to almost every triumph of
commerce or technology: the highest turnover, the biggest
tonnage, the fastest crossing, the greatest altitude, etc. Here,
a purely ludic element, for once, got the better of utilitar-
ian considerations, since the experts inform us that smaller
units – less monstrous steamers and aircrafts, etc. – are more
efficient in the long run. Business becomes play. This process goes so far that some of the great business concerns
deliberately instill the play-spirit into their workers so as to
step up production. The trend is now reversed: play becomes
business.

(Huizinga 1971 [1936]: 200)

Joyful colors, cartoons, jokes, toys, games and music can help
people to reactivate all the intelligence centers of the brain.
Getting back to the 'inner child' can greatly help to put more
joy into life, and especially into work.

(Jacqueline Miller 1997: 255)

Nearly 60 years separate these two quotes. The first quote is from
Huizinga's well-known book *Homo Ludens* (Playing man) in which
Huizinga studies play as a social phenomenon. A part of the book goes
on to explore ways in which play emerges in various areas of society
such as sports, politics and economy and it is here that he describes

the way in which financial organizations employ play in the form of competitions and records. The second quotation by Jacqueline Miller is from an article in which she argues in favour of modern organizations' increased use of play and humour. She describes play as an important resource in modern organizations. There is both continuity and discontinuity between the two quotations. There is continuity in their linking of play and organization. The discontinuity concerns the nature of this link. When Jacqueline Miller encourages organizations to use more play and humour, she is not concerned with competition as is the case in Huizinga, but instead with strengthening creativity, engagement and vitality. This continuity and discontinuity is the theme of this book. It focuses on the relations currently at play between organizations and play and also the significant unfolding of new forms of power.

Initially, my focus and interest were in an entirely different place. I was interested in the way in which modern organizations manage their employees and the way in which the public administration manages its citizens (Andersen & Born 2005). Personality has become an object of management in administrations in relation to its citizens as well as in organizations in relation to their employees. In today's public administration, the citizen is referred to as an active fellow citizen who is not simply the passive recipient of public services but is expected to assume responsibility for himself as citizen (Andersen 2003). In today's schools, students are expected to take on responsibility for their own learning (Knudsen 2007, 2008). The health care system expects of people that they take responsibility for a healthy lifestyle (Dahlager 2005). As a Norwegian Health Minister argued a few years ago, the citizen is expected to be his own Health Minister (Hydle 2003). It is no longer enough to simply do one's job in the workplace. Being concerned with one's duties is considered almost regressive. Today, we talk about the 'whole employee', who must be engaged, enterprising, flexible and adaptable (Andersen & Born 2001, 2007b, 2008). Following this trend, a range of new concepts and social technologies has emerged pertaining to issues of management of personality in both public administration and employment policies. Some of these are staff development interviews, performance appraisals, client conversations, parent classes, student plans, preventive conversations, personal profiles and citizens' contracts (Andersen 2007a, 2008b).

Over the past years I have collected material about such concepts, and I began to notice that more and more of these concepts and technologies were integrating play as an important element. In Denmark public schools have engaged in anti-bullying games. The Municipality of Copenhagen has been developing games about management and values. For many years, The Danish Road Safety Council has produced informative games about road safety and regulations for children and are currently developing reflective games for children and their parents, for example the board game *The bike race* and the game *Kasper and Split's new bikes* (Danish Road Safety Council 2006a, 2006b). The Centre for Voluntary Social Work has organized attitude games for volunteers. The National Board of Health has published games for young people entitled *Feel your way* about potential dilemmas associated with sex and emotions (National Board of Health 1999). However, this game was recalled by former Danish Health Minister Lars Løkke Rasmussen because of a complaint from a Christian free school. And finally, in the early 1990s, The Danish Crime Prevention Council began to develop different games intended in particular for use in public schools concerning social behaviour when going out and other youth related issues (Borch 2005: 150–152).

This fostered my interest in the role that play could perform in modern organizations and I began examine whether these examples represented unique occurrences or whether it was possible to trace a more significant trend. Once I began a systematic search on play and organization, I was struck by the magnitude, variation and prevalence of different types of play in organizations. Some focused on the management of employees and citizens. Also many other organizational themes were articulated through play such as innovation, strategy formation, teambuilding, quality management, diversity management and problem solving.

One example is a new concept at Lego. Lego is a well-known children's toy. However, Lego also has a concept called 'Lego Serious Play'. About this, they write: 'Lego Serious Play uses Lego bricks and elements and a unique method where people are empowered to "think through their fingers" – unleashing insight, inspiration and imagination' (http://www.seriousplay.com/8326/THE%20EXPERIENCE). In collaboration with, among other, Professor Davis Gauntlett from Bournemouth University, Lego has also developed a concept for consulting. The concept is described as a consultancy process that does not begin with a discussion of any   particular theme or problem. Instead, the problem is approached by using blocks to build and subsequently discuss: 'People build metaphors of their role and identity in a team or organization, then you get them to put it all together into one shared model, establishing the relationships between the different parts, all through working physically, and sharing it. By helping people to realize that they are themselves the true experts, team members feel genuine ownership of the insights that emerge' (Gauntlett 2006, for a more comprehensive description of Gauntlett's work with Lego: Gauntlett 2007). This concept is employed in educational establishments in relation to creative processes as well as in private companies in relation to management and teambuilding and in the social-political sector for purposes of building self-esteem among unemployed people. On the website for 'Lego serious play', one of the unemployed people from one of the projects stated: 'I think

Figure I.1   Girl power (www.artlab.org.uk/lego)

that people see me as friendly, loyal and honest. But in my Lego-identity model, we can see me as passionate and loyal, strong and disciplined, knowing where I am coming from and where I am going. A model can say a lot more about you than you can say about yourself. Building the model helped to see what person you really are – I chose the elephant to show that I am a stronger person than others think I am' (http://www.artlab.org.uk/legofieldwork.htm). According to the website, the Lego figure shown in Figure I.1 expresses the concept of 'girl power' by associating the tiger with the female figure and the colour pink (http://www.artlab.org.uk/lego.htm).

Another example is the way in which Danish Gymnastics and Sports Associations employ sports games as a way to solve conflicts between fighting ethnic groups in war-ridden areas such as the Balkans as an alternative relief aid. They have organized Open Football Schools in Bosnia-Herzegovina as a way to break the ice, by restoring playing and speaking terms among children and adults from different ethnic groups, who had found themselves on opposing sides in the war (Bille 2005). On an international level, this type of work is based in the organization Right to Play, which was established in 2003.

A third example is the game *Responsibility across boundaries*, which is produced by Zentropa for The Regional Networks for Companies' Social Involvement. This game is intended for small and medium-sized companies. It is a so-called dialogue game without losers and winners and without universal advice or prewritten recommendations. The game encourages dialogue about issues of social responsibility for companies in relations to themes such as refugees and immigrants, stress, particularly vulnerable groups, bullying, sickness and health. Players are invited to a discussion of ideal solutions versus practical solutions in relation to an imagined company (Regional Networks for Companies' Social Involvement 2005).

This tendency towards new links between play and organization has generally been overlooked in social studies internationally. However, some literature exists. Costea *et al.* (2006) study the conceptual–historical relationship between play and work over the past 25 years focusing on play as a means to introduce happiness and wellbeing into work (what I will later refer to as the 'for fun' strategy). Their point is: 'Organizational life becomes a site for the search for "personal wellness", a place and time where "well-being" is defined and self-expression actively encouraged, where "happiness" is sought through a proliferation of techniques celebrating the self. The "private" and the "public", "work" and "play", "production" and "consumption", "work on work" and "work of self" are amalgamated in a new and subtle way. It seems that, after a hundred years of apparently very rational, "Apollonian" approaches to efficiency and productivity, management itself has entered into a kind of "Dionysian" mode, a spirit of playful transgression and destruction of boundaries, a new bond between economic grammars of production and consumption, and cultural grammars of the modern self. This, we argue, is what might lie behind the increased use of ludic technologies in management' (Costea *et al.* 2005: 141, Costea *et al.* 2006). Similarly, Peter Fleming has written an article that focuses on what he refers to as 'for fun' cultural programmes. His main point is that these fun programmes function on one hand to help dissolve boundaries between work and non-work, but that on the other hand the programs involve a significant level of cynicism, which means that fun is not all that fun after all (Fleming 2005).

In addition, there exist a small number of articles celebrating the inherent vitality and virtualization capacity of play as a phenomenon and its transgression of linear rationality. Play is basically perceived as a phenomenon of critical transgression, which is a notion that can be traced back to Marx and his analysis of work and alienation (Marx 1964: 89). One such article is 'Dreams of time, times of dreams: Stories of creation from role-playing game sessions' by Jerzy Kociatkiewicz. Kociatkiewicz studies so-called role-playing in which participants, directed by a game master, create a story and cause the game to move along. The starting point for the game is an 'empty space', which the participants fill through their discussions and actions throughout the game. Kociatkiewicz's point is that the game establishes a creative, poetic and non-linear self-organization, which modern organizations can learn from, particularly with respect to the question of creativity (Kociatkiewicz 2000). Another example is Daniel Hjort, who connects entrepreneurship closely together with organizational spaces for learning and inventions. Daniel Hjort concludes: 'If management cannot learn to live with *homo ludens* as neighbour, it is difficult to see a role for management in organizational entrepreneurship' (Hjort 2004: 430). A third article 'Ideas are born in fields of play: Towards a theory of play and creativity in organizational settings' by Charalampos Mainemelis and Sarah Ronson. In it they perceive play as the cradle of creativity. They distinguish between two functions of play in organizations. Play can function as distancing in relation to work, e.g. when employees sometimes play football at work. In that case, play has a social, environment-building function. Or play can create engagement when work and its premises becomes the object of play. This gives play an innovative function. They write: 'the role of play is not to abolish purpose, consistency, and rationality from organizational life; rather, the role of play is to help organizations maintain more flexible and sophisticated forms of consistency by encouraging their members to occasionally experiment with possible realities, behaviours, or identities' (Mainemelis & Ronson 2006).

Other articles concern spontaneous play in the workplace. John Bowman points out the need for a work sociology that is also a play sociology. His acknowledges that many people already play at work: 'Spontaneous play and games are a characteristic part of some work experiences, and workers routinely manage to blend both work and play' (Bowman 1987: 66).

Whereas play seems to enter the organization and work in new forms, recent research on computer and online games, such as *Second Life*, indicates that work, in turn, becomes an element in play. As computer games have grown into an independent medium, several new research journals focusing on games have emerged, including the journal *Games and Culture*, which focuses on the cultural and social consequences of the growing consumption of computer and online games (Steinkuehler 2006, Lowood 2006). In an issue of this journal, Nick Yee has written an article entitled 'The labour of fun' in which he describes how many online players view these games as their 'other job'. The players describe their games as a responsibility. One player says: 'Was more like work than fun. One day got burnt out trying to get exp for level 55 and quit' (Yee 2006: 69). Yee's thesis is that 'video games play important roles in the increasingly blurred intersections of our social, economic, and political spheres, and articulating those blurred boundaries in the microcosm of video games reveals larger trends in our digitally mediated world' (Yee 2006: 68) He concludes: 'Ultimately, the blurring work and play begs the question – what does fun really mean?' (Yee 2006: 71).

Play has always taken place, and in segmented societies play has been linked to specific rituals, e.g. initiation rituals. Since the end of the 1800s, a number of books have been written about games from an anthropological perspective (Roth 1976 [1902], Groos 1976 [1901],

Caillois 1982 [1958], Eifermann 1970). Several of these books perceive play as a universal phenomenon and study play in different primitive societies. Therefore, there is a substantial amount of literature about play in American Indian cultures and Inuit societies. Moreover, some of these books study play among monkeys and draw parallels to the games in American Indian culture. That falls outside the area of interest of the present book, but it is interesting to observe a renewed interest in the games of segmented societies. Today's designers of games for modern organizations see these games from segmented societies as a kind of innovation reservoir, almost in the same way that alternative medicine sees untouched rain forests. One example is Michael Brown's article 'The bone game: A ritual of transformation' from a journal on experimental learning. Brown asks what we can learn from Native Americans with respect to promoting personal development. He points out that rituals in native people contain many forms of insight that we need today. The article analyses an example called 'Bone Game'. This game was played among tribes or groupings within tribes when conflicts came to a head and threatened to cause wars or other aggressions. It is a fairly complex game. An important characteristic of the game is the size of the stakes. The winner gets what the other party has gambled, and the stakes are typically so large that they fundamentally question the very nature of winning and losing. The tribe might for example gamble its entire food stock for the winter or all its hunting tools. That means that losing threatens the survival of the tribe and forces the tribe to reconsider the tribe and develop its inner resources On the other hand, as the winner, the tribe not only becomes very wealthy, but also receives an enormous responsibility in relation to the losing tribe. The loser has become life-dependent on the winner and that puts the winner under a certain level of obligation. Brown sums it up in this way: 'The ritual enlivens the individuals who play it, helps them get in touch with imagination, intuition, creativity, and insight, and creates powerful bonds between them. Many lessons are learned from this game about the differences between competition and cooperation, fear and courage, timidity and power, deception and honesty, attachment and transcendence' (Brown 1990: 49). This game has been adapted and employed by a number of modern organizations, voluntary organization, public authorities, and universities in America and Canada.

The present book focuses on the relation between organization and play. Its general thesis is the extent to which the new focus on play is connected to the fact that conditions for the exercise of power have changed. The book discusses the way in which play has been turned into a power technology in modern, flexible and adaptable organizations.

What interests me, therefore, is not play in itself. It is also not simply play in organizations. What interest me are organizational games as a symptom of changing conditions for organizational and political power. The book is not about what games do well or not so well. It is also not about whether play is capable of promoting learning, innovation and creativity. The epistemological interest of the book pertains to diagnostics of present and enquires into reasons why play has exploded over the past 15 years in private, public and voluntary organizations, and what is put at stake in this explosion. This includes, not least, the way in which play allows for decision and power to become coupled together and the implications of this.

I do not argue that there is anything new about the fact that power and play become coupled together. My assertion is that this coupling has taken on different qualities today due to radical changes in organizational conditions. The productivity of power has been displaced. For example, the governmentality discussion points to the emergence of various empowerment logics where all management becomes the management of self-management (Dean 2007). As a parallel trend, the governance discussions indicate the way in which steering turns into supervision of self-steering and monolithic hierarchies dissolve into polycentrism (Newman 2001, Clarke & Newman 1997, Andersen 1995). The general trend is the dissolution of the almost classical conception of hierarchical chains of power and relations of inferiority and superiority. Another general development is the notion that power as a medium of communication ends up standing in the way of power itself. We used to speak about 'distributed power' in the organization, which sought to increase its power by delegating power. Today it is more radical. The very activity of delegating power implies that power becomes more visible which means that it becomes an obstacle to itself. Today's ideal is about constant change without relinquishing alternative forms of change. It is the situational decision, which is unimpeded by prescribed premises. Today's decision premises are ascribed to the decision once it has been made. The organization as the creator of premises is increasingly becoming an artefact ascribed to a multiplicity of decisions.

The book raises the following questions:

1. In which ways are the relation between organization and play articulated and how, in these articulations, is play assigned functions as organizationally creative? I show that, since the end of the 1800s, a new organizational language has emerged, which articulates play as an important part of modern organization and management. From the 1980s on, this turns into a language about play as an organizational force of self-organization. Thus, play is linked to organization as the core of organization in the organization's creation of itself as an organization and as the core in employees' creation of themselves, both as people and employees.

2. How is play as a form of communication linked to decision as a form of communication, and how does that impact an organizations' presentation of its unity? I show that play and decision represent two heterogeneous forms of communication each with their own logic. Moreover, I show that modern organizational games can be seen as an attempt on behalf of the organizations to free themselves from themselves as a barrier to change and instead establish an integrational form that allows for a multiplicity of difference without threatening the organizational unity.

3. How does play define constitutive boundaries in today's political system through games, e.g. the boundaries administration/citizen, individual/community and state/institution? I point to a number of games, which have been developed in order to manage citizens, parents, volunteers, etc. Today, many public institutions seek to manage with respect to issues that fall outside their formal domains, which is precisely where the validity of power communication ceases to apply. The designing of games represents such a strategy. Organizational games are about power that does not wish to be power, or does not wish to look like power. Today, play represents a technology for self-management in organizations, where power runs up against its own wall.

4. How do new organizational games lead to new links between play, pedagogy and power? Which form does power take on when seeking to assert itself through play? I show that play is first pedagogized and then the pedagogical turns playful, which means that

power as a form is doubled as power and empowerment, which renders the logic of power invisible in a new way.

The book's structure can be summed up like this:

Object: Organizational

Guiding lines:
The semantic history of management games

The organization at play

Political creation games

The power of play

Problem: How does play come into being as organizational and political practice and which concept of power does this produce?

Sub-problem 1: In which way is the relation play/organization articulated and how is play assigned organizationally creative functions?

Sub-problem 2: How is the form of communication of play and decision respectively defined? In which ways do they become linked in modern creation games? And what are the implications of this for the conditions for the production of organizational unity?

Sub-problem 3: In which way does play currently challenge constitutive boundaries in the political system, e.g. the boundaries administration/citizen and state/institution?

Sub-problem 4: In which way do new organizational games encourage new links between play, pedagogy, and power? What form does power take on when seeking to assert itself?

Figure I.2 General problem

1
Second-order Observation

This book is based on a specific epistemology and a specific concept of observation, which embraces a programme about observing observations as observations.

Niklas Luhmann defines observation as an indication within the framework of a difference (Luhmann 1993d). All observations operate by virtue of a difference. When an observation fastens upon something in the world, a difference is made between this 'something' and everything else. What the observer sees is only indicated and visible in the observation in relation to that which it is distinguished from. This means that the difference indicates how observation takes place. A game, for example, is always a game to an observer. There are different ways in which a game becomes visible in an observation. There is a difference between observing through the differences of: fun/not fun; educationally better/worse; and pay/not pay. In the first observation, a game becomes an invitation to play, in the second a pedagogical form, and in the third a commodity.

The point is that each observation is an operation which draws a difference, and that difference is not visible to the observation itself. The observation always indicates one side of the difference and leaves the other side unmarked and yet constitutive in the observation. One sees what one sees, but one does not see the perspective and the difference through which one sees. Thus, the difference defines the blind spot of the observation.

With reference to Spencer-Brown, Luhmann refers to the inside of the difference as the marked side (m) and the outside of the difference as the unmarked side (Spencer-Brown 1969; see also Robertson

m

Form

Figure 1.1 The form calculus

1999). The blind spot constitutes the very unity of the difference, that which both divides the two sides and holds them together in one difference. This is called the form of difference and can be formalized as in Figure 1.1.

An observation, indicating something in the world cannot also indicate itself. However, a new observation is able to observe the observation. This observation is able to observe both the fact that something is indicated and the difference within which the indication takes place. Therefore, it is able to observe the blind spot of the first observation. That is the epistemological programme of Luhmann's systems theory: to observe the blind spots of other observations. This is called second-order observation (Luhmann 1993d).

Observing in the second order means to observe observations as observations. That means that what we articulate about the 'observations' as objects of our study also applies to the articulation itself. Second-order observation is simultaneously first-order observation, and takes place, therefore, within the framework of a difference. Thus, it is not a privileged position of observation, poised above other observations. The conditions that apply to first-order observation apply to second-order observations as well. The theory of observation encompasses itself, so to speak. The difference through which second-order observation observes is the difference indication/difference. Therefore, an observation can be formalized as the unity of the difference (see Figure 1.2).

This means that second-order observations are highly reductionistic. Second-order observations are only able to see indications and differences, nothing else! Second-order observation is not a pursuit of the general staff of observations. Observations must be observed as such in their immediate scarcity and not as something else, and this is precisely what makes systems theory so capable of deactivating

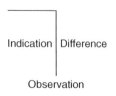

Figure 1.2 Observation as form

banalities. It represents a form of neoconcretism. It is an insistence upon the effort to stay with the observations and not immediately move towards their context of causes or meaning. Observations are not to be interpreted. Their meaning is not to be unfolded. They are also not to be explained. They are merely to be described and diagnosed: What is the difference used to observe? How is the blind spot defined? How can new observations be added? This is the way I use the form shown in Figure 1.1 and symbolized for future reference as (⌐). It compels me to stay with the individual distinction, to maintain and observe it.

1. Communication

I am not interested in all forms of observation operations. My focus is organizational communication. I don't observe the way in which individuals observe play, power and organization. I am interested in the communicative observations in organizations.

I do not understand communication to be a specific form of action where a sender sends a message to a recipient, and where communication is perceived as successful once the recipient understands the message as it was intended by the sender. By contrast, in systems theoretical terms communication is defined as a network of retrospective connections. What does that mean? When something is said, connectivity is established. Connectivity is a horizon of possible links by new communicative operations. For example, someone makes a sarcastic statement about something to a colleague. Potentially, however, that statement opens up many possible future connections, which might take further communication in many different directions. Perhaps, the statement gets no response; that is, no connection has been established and hence no further communication develops. Perhaps the colleague connects with the communication on the premise of being included by the sarcasm, perhaps the colleague connects with the communication from the point of view of a literal interpretation or perhaps the sarcastic statement is maintained by a joke. The point is that whether or not communication takes place cannot be determined until the connection is made by a second statement, and of equal importance is that it is also not until the occurrence of the second statement that the second-order observer can define the character of the communication as serious, literal or witty. Thus, communication is fundamentally different from acts of speech. In this perspective, communication consists not of acts of speech but of selection, where connections to a horizon of connectivity produce new connectivity thus opening up new connections, etc. Communication cannot be reduced to the acts of speech of the communication participants but has a life of its own, which no individual participant is able to control. Consider a meeting: A manager may make elaborate plans as to the process of the meeting and yet the agenda slips. Issues that should have remained untouched are opened up, and issues that should have been discussed only briefly turn out to open up to unexpected connectivity. In the end, however, the right decisions are agreed upon as anticipated, but at the next meeting when the minutes are to be approved, it turns out that what was considered a clear decision is subsequently decided to be merely a discussion.

In social systems, operations of observation and system formation happen through communication. Social systems consist of communication and nothing but communication. Communication represents a threefold operation: (i) information selection (what information to pass on); (ii) utterance selection (how to pass on information) and; (iii) understanding selection (how to understand the message). There is no communication without the occurrence of all three aspects. Not until a link is established in relation to the message, e.g. through understanding, can there be communication. Monologues are not communication. However, we should not perceive of understanding in terms of psychology. Understanding does not imply the way in which a system of consciousness incorporates the message into it. It only implies the way in which subsequent communication links up with it. Every message opens up a multitude of possible connections. A message can perhaps be understood, that is, linked up to, as humorous, literal, inviting, dictating, etc. There is always a surplus of connectivity. In terms of systems theory, understanding is defined as the selection of a link in relation to the horizon of possibilities for linking. Until a link is made, there is no communication. In this way, communication is established retrospectively or recursively. It is always the subsequent communication that decides whether communication takes place and how. Every link itself opens up a new horizon of possible linking and does not become communication until a new link makes a selection from these, etc. Moreover, that means that no one is able to control communication. Communication participants cannot decide the continuation of the communication. In this sense, communication leads a life 'of is own'. Luhmann defines social systems as autopoietical systems that create themselves from communication as a network of recursive operations (Luhmann 2000, for a critique of Luhmann's concept of autopoiesis: Münch 1992).

In other words, social systems can be perceived as a net of recursive communication, which, by means of operations of distinction, create, stabilize or displace expectations concerning the continuation of the communication. When a statement such as 'she is sweet' is not only thought but said, it creates expectations concerning the continuation of the communication. The recipient expects that the sender expects that the recipient either confirms or disproves the statement. The recipient is not expected to reply, for example: 'Have you heard the weather forecast for tomorrow?' But the recipient can never be sure to know the expectations of the sender. In the statement 'she is sweet' only the marked side is visible, and 'sweet' can potentially imply the actualization of a number of differences such as sweet/unpleasant, sweet/sour, sweet/unsexy, sweet/smart. Not until one of the differences, e.g. sweet/sour, has been confirmed does the difference stabilize communication participants' expectations with respect to the communication's continuation. Thus, differences establish not only individual observations but also communicative observations perceived as expectations with respect to the communication's continuation. Differences create possibilities for coupling and horizons within which the communication can move.

A social system consists of pure actuality, of communicative operations, which continually disappear and which only momentarily make connections recursively to other operations. Each communicative operation either confirms and condenses the previous communication or displaces the formative movement and enables the emergence of a new system of communication with a new set of expectations with regard to the continuation of the communication (Clam 2000). Thus, a communication initiation can either (1) be *confirmed* so that the communication is continued on the marked side of the communication-guiding difference, (2) be *contradicted* so that the difference is crossed and the communication is continued in the same form but on the unmarked side, (3) be *displaced* so that a new difference is inserted with a new set of possible links, or (4), be *discontinued* so that no link is made and no new horizon of expectations is established. []] is not just a difference framing the way in which something is observed, it is also a difference that creates expectations with respect to the possible continuation of the communication.

This also means that autopoietical social systems are operatively closed. This closedness is inherent in the very split mechanism of the operations; the fact that these are operations with two sides, which means that subsequent operations can only link up to one or the other side or change form and take on a new distinction, which simply means the formation of a new system. The economic system of communication, for example, operates within the form to pay/not pay, and the continuation of the economic communication can only take place through an act of payment or non-payment. Economic communication cannot be continued by means of a declaration of love. That would not represent a recursive link but instead a displacement of the form and hence the potential formation of a different system of communication.

When I emphasize the fact that communication leads a life of its own which no individual communication participant is able to control, I also argue for the analytical productivity of a razor-sharp distinction between systems of communication and systems of consciousness. Systems of consciousness can participate in communication, but they cannot communicate with one another. Systems of consciousness are not able to recursively link up with each other's operations. That would equal mind-reading. In fact we can argue that communication is only possible precisely because systems of consciousness are unable to link up with each other's operations. There is a difference between what a system of consciousness states and what it thinks it wants to state. If both sides were visible, communication would rapidly break down. A person often does not state his or her truthful opinion of someone else. It is one thing to think that the other person is an idiot. It is something else to say it. If both the actual statement and the thought were available as a possible link to the other person, communication would break down. A system of consciousness can link up with communication, but communication can only link up with other communication. Only communication is able to communicate. Systems of consciousness are condemned to functioning as the environment of communication. In analytical-strategic terms, this is a question, as we have already mentioned, of maintaining that operations of observation have to be observed precisely as observations. It is a question of being concrete in relation to communication as operations and not be persuaded to move one's focus onto the communication participants but to observe communication in its capacity of communication without reducing it to individual motives and intentions, which are invisible in the communication and which the observer can only imagine: hence the importance of the razor-sharp distinction.

There exists a multitude of more specific analytical strategies for conducting second-order observation, both within and outside the framework of systems theory. I have chosen to introduce these as they are relevant in the book. The point of departure for my inquiry into the relationship between power and play is fundamentally that I do not ask whether this or that game is actual play. I am also not interested in discussing whether power distorts or manipulates play, or whether playing is a good thing. I remain at the distanced second-order level where I take the liberty to simply ask how communication takes place.

2
The Semantic History of Management Games

Introduction

We can begin a second-order observation with this question: How have play and games made their way into organizations? The first time I came across examples of play and games for organizations, I was convinced that I had encountered something entirely new. But nothing is ever entirely new. There are only displacements.

Moreover, if a social phenomenon is studied in its current form, there is the risk that the language used to describe the phenomenon is unable to rise above the phenomenon's topical self-description. The analysis becomes nothing more than an aspect of the observed object. The distance necessary in order to observe is not achieved. The analysis becomes nothing more than a reflection of the topicality of the phenomenon. In order not to become a prisoner of the same discursive prison as the phenomenon it is important to enquire into the historical origins of the phenomenon and its previous forms. Thus, from a second-order perspective, a good place to begin is to always enquire into the semantic history of the phenomenon, that is, a study of the concepts through which the phenomenon initially emerged.

Semantic analysis is a second-order observation which employs the distinction concept–meaning (Luhmann 1993c). The semantic analysis looks at the way in which meaning and expectations are condensed into concepts and are stored for communication as needed.

A concept is constituted from the condensation and generalization of a multiplicity of meanings and expectations. A concept *condenses* expectations in a way so that many different kinds of expectations are included. 'Play' has different expectations from 'work'. The use of a specific concept in communication establishes expectations about expectations of the communication. Furthermore, concepts are *general* in the sense that a concept is never identical with its particular use in a particular communication. The concept is generally available to communication, but in communication it obtains a specific meaning and actualizes specific expectations.

The concept of 'state', for example, links together a large number of meaning elements such as taxation, territory, legal exertion of power, bureaucracy and citizenship. The multiplicity of meaning in the form of a concept is always instructed by the distinction between concept and counter-concept. This is shown in Figure 2.1.

There can be no concept without a counter-concept, which functions to keep the concept in its place. The counter-concept establishes certain restrictions for the concept. One conceptual pair is play/seriousness in which the meaning condensed into the concept of 'seriousness' establishes certain restrictions for the meaning of 'play'. The expectations associated with seriousness establish restrictions for what can be expected of a situation, which is indicated as play in the communication.

In relation to this, semantics refers to the store of concepts that is available for communication. The semantic analysis distinguishes between three dimensions of meaning. The *social dimension* is the dimension in the semantic construction of social identity in which there exists only one 'us' (concept) in relation to one 'them' (counter-concept). 'Us' is only us as in its difference to 'them', however, 'them' exists only to the extent that 'us' refers to 'them'. This means that expectations of 'others' define the limit for expectations of 'ourselves'. The *factual dimension* is the dimension in the semantic construction of factual relations in which 'things' are ordered in relation to one another and in relation to 'us'. Finally, the *temporal dimension* is the

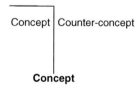

Figure 2.1 The concept of concept

dimension for the construction of 'us-in-time', where any present is always suspended between the future (concept) and the past (counter-concept). The future represents a horizon of expectations and the past a space of experience, and any present is constituted solely by the tension between these. Concepts about, for example, the past and future of social policy define its present form and topical compulsion to act. The three dimensions can be formalized as shown in Figure 2.2.

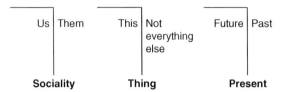

Figure 2.2   Semantic dimension

Thus, in deciding upon a semantic analytical strategy, the questions are: How are meaning and expectations established? How do these becomes condensed or generalized in concepts? Which semantic store do these concepts establish for systems of communication? This includes the question of how concepts become displaced to produce new counter-concepts, or counter-concepts become the counter-concept for a new concept, or the counter-concept becomes unspecific, which leads to a battle to fill it.

My thesis is that the relation between organization, game and play has undergone a number of fundamental semantic shifts over the past century. I believe that it is possible to distinguish between at least the three different semantic phases shown in Table 2.1.

Considering such radical shifts, the material for the analysis naturally varies over time. The textual forms of semantics changes in accordance with changes in semantics are large. On a very general level, I distinguish between two forms of material. The first form

Table 2.1   Time period

Time period	Play in organizations
From 1860	Competitive games
From 1955	Training and simulation games
From 1980	Social creation games

consists of texts that articulate the relation between play and organization, and the second consists of directions for and descriptions of specific games and forms of play. I have looked generally for the concepts of play and organization in their broadest sense. My point of departure has not been a specific definition of play as a measure of relevance, but instead what has empirically speaking been associated and not associated with play. I also have not limited myself in a narrow sense to the term play, but have tried to remain open to many different terms of equivalency, e.g. game, competition, match, etc.

From the 1860s onwards, there are a number of articulations of the relation between play and organization, but up until around 1920 the material is rather sporadic. Generally, I have used rather broad search criteria. I have focused on international material as well as from Denmark where I have a more privileged access. I have searched in more generally accessible material as well as in practice-based business journals and business literature.

Starting in the 1950s, one can trace the emergence of an international discourse about management games. The discourse is international in its character with large numbers of international conferences. At this point in time, the material consists primarily of international research journals, compilations of conference papers and a number of books and articles about the games under development. The discourse appears fairly coherent and, moreover, relates specifically to discourse within business economics.

From the beginning of the 1980s, the very internationally-based discourse is still visible, but it is no longer as closely linked to a specific discourse within business economics. The discourse appears no longer to be centred on international research journals. Instead, what dominates in this period are consultancy-based books filled with directions and recipes for games. Moreover, these consultants are not just business economists – many of them are psychologists and social workers. Thus, we see in this phase a return to a higher level of heterogeneity although it is also characterized by strong regularity.

1. The semantics of competition and records

In a Danish context, the initial articulations of the relation between play and organization date back to the mid-1800s and are a part of the institutional framework surrounding cattle shows and industrial exhibitions. At cattle shows and industrial exhibitions (e.g. the so called 'worlds fairs' such as the International Exhibition of 1862), manufacturers displayed their most advanced products, technology and craftsmanship.

In themselves, these fairs comprise a playful element. They represent both a form of marketing and a kind of physical reconstruction of the market as meeting place, but a market which is not the market itself. Instead it offers a simulated and symbolic market, which provides a simplified description of the market and of the manufacturers' reflection in one another, in the knowledge that this is different from the market as it normally works. As noted by a writer for a Danish Newspaper in 1862 in connection with the International Exhibition in London, the difference between exhibition and real life is comparable to the difference between someone's Sunday dress and everyday dress (*Illustreret Tidende* 1862: 342). Economic markets do not have an address, voice or appearance. These exhibitions are meant to reflect the market, but they are not the market. The products at the exhibitions are not the same as the one currently on the market but represent, at best, products that might become available on the market in the future.

Real market economy is characterized by competition. This element is present in symbolic form at the exhibitions in the form of competitions and prizes. These represent a form of 'play-competition and play-pricing', but at the same time it is not pure play since they refer back to the competition of the real world and the serious business that precedes the exhibitions and the fact that a prize can be transformed into capital in the competition that follows once the exhibitions are over. At the cattle shows, farmers compete for the best breeding animals. *Illustreret Tidende* (1861) published the picture of the bull that was assigned the royal prize (see Figure 2.3).

There were also competitions and prizes at the industrial exhibitions. At the Nordic Exhibition in Copenhagen in 1872, the King attended the exhibition and presented the prizes. *Illustreret Tidende* wrote: 'On this occasion, our King once again showed his great interest in this national matter and had assumed responsibility for giving away the medals and diplomas. At a set time, the entire royal family appeared among the crowds of participants dressed in gala. A celebratory march opens the ceremony whereupon His Excellency the President thanked his Majesty the King for presenting the

Figure 2.3   The royal prize bull
Source: *Illustreret Tidende*, årg. 2, no. 98, 11/8–1861, s. 370 (http://img.kb.dk/iti/02/pdf/
iti_02_0368.pdf)

prizes' (*Illustreret Tidende* 1872: 470, my translation). The newspaper
published a picture of the event as shown in Figure 2.4.

These two examples indicate that the competitions and prize-giving
do not simply symbolize the competition of market economy. They
also involve a national and class-related symbolism. The market does
not talk and cannot be represented. A market is horizontal. It has
no hierarchical top. In this context, however, the King is assigned
a higher level of authority. The nation speaks as a substitute for the
market and authoritatively assigns prizes and status.

This kind of link to royalty gradually disappears throughout the
1900s as groups of managers and CEOs as well as professional organizations took control of the organising of the competitions. The tradition for presenting prizes is carried on. The Nobel Prize began in 1900
and the Pulitzer Prize in 1917. According to Neil Borden (1925), the
first few decades of the 1900s produce a wealth of prizes, even though
most of them have the character of one-time-deals. As a result, we see
an emerging discussion and literature concerning 'methods of reward-
ing' (Bok 1925: 435–445). Neil Borden (1925) discusses the principles
of decent prize-giving in relation to the founding of Harvard Advertising Awards in 1924. He considers prize-giving a form of competition,
which should abide by clear rules and regulations. To be given a prize

Figure 2.4   Nordic Exhibition in Copenhagen 1872 (from *Illustreret Tidende* 1872: 470)

is to win a prize. A prize is not to be given as a royal favour but should be based on the objective assessment of a professionally made-up jury with reference to public, clear and calculable criteria. However, competition is not to take place solely for the sake of competition. Neil Borden believes that there are two general purposes of competition-based awards. One is to encourage the individual employee (or company), where the award is considered a visual recognition of someone who has done well. The second purpose is educational: 'Yet the awards provoke interest, discussion, and thought and thus serve educationally by centering attention and study upon worthwhile work' (Borden 1925: 259). The hope is that such education will establish a standard for the market. Competition with an element of play is initiated in order to discipline the competition of the markets.

However, competition also gains a footing within the individual company. In 1924, *Harvard Business Review* (1924b) published an article with the title 'The use of contest among salesmen'. This article immediately followed an article about wage-based reward systems, which sought to find the most optimal wage system, which would increase competition among employees while guaranteeing employees fundamental security in the form of a fixed base pay (*Harvard Business Review* 1924a: 474–480). However, the article about salesmanship is not about daily competition but about the occasional use of contests without any financial rewards attached, which are thought to stimulate company morale. These contests, thus, function as a form of play in the organization and are intended to strengthen a competitive mindset and examine what can be achieved when employees do their very best. This article was based on an empirical study of 171 companies using this form of competition. The article explores different ways of organizing contests and their effects on efficiency and morale. The article concludes: 'Contests are of value in meeting special situations and in building up morale particular in large organizations. . . . While the effect on the salespeople and sales is good during the life of the contest, the effect after the contests are completed is doubtful. Moreover, sales contests offer many opportunities for hard feeling and suspicion between men and the management, and inefficiencies may creep into the organization from causes which have been pointed out. Sales contests, then, should be introduced only after careful study of special conditions to determine the suitable form and after some really equitable basis has been devised for making allowances for differences between men and territories' (*Harvard Business Review* 1924b: 489).

From the 1920s on, awards and contests also appear in product advertising. Basically, this means that the customer is given an additional gift when purchasing a product, a gift that generally has no relation to the product. There might be music recordings included with a pack of cigarettes, lottery tickets in cereal products, or coupons for which one receives a prize after collecting a certain number of them. This establishes a form of contest, which is unrelated to the product. It is a contest tied to actual competition in that it seeks to stabilize sales and unite customers with a particular brand. At the same time, however, these contests and awards offer the consumer a meaning, which is more about play than seriousness, a form of super-serious meaning. And when perceived from a fair competition point of view, it has the appearance of unfair play (Sommer 1932: 203–210).

Personnel management is yet another area where competitive games are discussed and studied. At the centre of the discussions is the concept of motivation: What motivates an employee? Julius Maller represents a more radical position. He writes: 'To talk of abso-lutely unmotivated work is to admit response without stimulus or effect without course' (Maller 1929: 1). Philip Cabot notes somewhat more philosophically: 'Competition produces imaginative activity and forces a man to take a risk. The men in competitive industry are like men crossing a river filled with floating ice cakes; each leap is a desperate but necessary venture' (Cabot 1925: 387). However, many people emphasize a more differentiated concept of motivation, which also includes positive and non-monetary motivations, and in that context a number of activities that include aspects of play are articulated, not least internal contests.

Clarck Dickinson is among those who seek to develop an eye for 'non-pecuniary incentives'. He considers it a problem that a lot of modern industrial organization of work results in reduced efficiency because routine work leads to boredom, which causes people to day-dream and accidents to happen. Therefore, one specific goal becomes to distract boredom and as part of that effort he emphasizes 'joy in work': 'It may well be true of many or most people that they would be happiest if not obliged to work at all; yet if they must work, they will becomes most effective in those jobs which are most nearly enjoyable (Dickinson 1937: 432). He later introduces what he refers to as 'the hobby nexus (between worker and work)' (Dickinson 1937: 452). He raises the question of what makes a hobby, and his answer is that a hobby is 'a systematic, cumulative sort of play' (Dickinson 1937: 452). On this basis he reflects upon whether work might even become a 'source of pleasure' (Dickinson 1937: 453). He pays particular atten-tion to the introduction of competitions: 'Nearly every one likes some

competitive sports or games, including various degrees of gambling;
and this spirit not seldom gives rise to spontaneous races in production among operatives in a workshop, even when no material gain
for themselves is in question' (Dickinson 1937: 445). He discusses at
length ways in which to develop internal award systems intended for
employees who make a particular effort and particular for employees
or employee collectives who bring up good ideas and suggestions to
the management, e.g. about how to improve equipment or reduce
waste. He is enthralled by the possibilities associated with the use of
formal decoration or certificates of honour for individual employees
or collectives. He finds a great deal of inspiration in the development
in the Soviet Union and in what is referred to as 'socialist competition'. He quotes a Moscow News report from May 1 1934: 'It is not
only the workers who are engaged in socialist contest. The cooks in
the four dining halls of that same plant challenged each other to pre-
pare better meals, while the waitresses compete with each other as
to who can serve more hungry workers in one shift … From simple
rivalry between two workers, socialist competition has grown until
it has becomes an All Union affair, embracing tens of thousands of
mines, mills, farms and plants' (Dickinson 1937: 445). In Soviet competitions, awards are given in the form of money, vacations and other
privileges, and one might be assigned the Order of Lenin or become
the Hero of Workers. He also describes similar systems in America. His
conclusion is: 'Competition may undoubtedly give extra zest to work'
(Dickinson 1937: 446).

Several other people think along the same lines. Professors Richard
Lansburgh and William Spriegel identify the building of morale as
an important aspect of organization and management, and they
believe that recreational and athletic activities in companies can add
to such morale building. They give examples such as lunch speeches,
concerts, annual balls and basketball as activities that build morale
(Lansburgh & Spriegel 1940: 333–334). However, such activities can
also be exaggerated, e.g. basketball is no longer a productive activity because it causes an exaggerated focus on competition. The book
Personnel Management discusses the nature of work and is interested
in what aspect of hobbies causes people to go back to work after a
long day of 'real' work. The answer is that a hobby is play, and play
is driven by fundamentally different motives from work: 'Play is different from work in that play is essentially the end in itself, whereas

work is a means to an end. The incentive to play is the pleasure itself derived from playing the game or whatever it may be' (Scott, Clothier, Mathewson & Spriegel 1941: 304). Emphasizing competitions and recreational activities in companies can strengthen the desire to work and promote general well-being.

Company sports have their own history and emerge as organized athletic competitions between companies. In Denmark, there are sports clubs associated with particular companies that date back to 1860, but actual company sports where company teams compete against each other are not established until the 1920s. The trend started in the banking and insurance world but quickly spread into the crafts and industries, and in 1921, the first Danish company sports association, FKBU, was formed (Sørensen 1980: 205). Company sports have always distinguished themselves from other sports. They have not perceived themselves as elitist sports but have associated their efforts with other goals, which are perhaps expressed in the following verse from 1941 (Janner 1971:13, translated from Danish):

And fellowship is our first command
which shall forever be honoured between us
it shall be carried from our workplaces
to any sports ground
and there our strength will be tried.
As comrades we return
to the day's work, hand in hand we go
rejuvenated towards new work days

The verse dates back to a prologue by the Danish writer Aage Herman, which he wrote in connection with the twentieth anniversary of the company sports association HKBU. Here, the purpose of company sports is to strengthen the sense of fellowship in a workplace by testing it in the context of competitions outside the workplace, and subsequently, the experiences from this test are brought back to the workplace in the form of a rejuvenated sense of fellowship. In the song's other verses, company sports are seen as 'competition of peace'. The prologue speaks of 'sports games', which instil in us the proper 'sports spirit' according to which one can only win through 'honourable play'. Company sports are defined as training for competitive skills so that a competitive mentality is at once strengthened and disciplined. The types of sports typically included in company sports at this point were mostly team sports, particularly soccer, and company sports were concerned with the ability to compete and team development. Or as it says in the first verse of the prologue, the athlete always strives 'in carefree sports games ... to give the team everything one has got' (Janner 1971: 13, my translation).

Thus, from the 1860s on we see the emergence of a broad range of competitive games in companies and other organizations. These games represent organized play between companies, between employees and between consumers. The articulation of these games appears to define two distinctions. One is the distinction between competition and play. The other distinction is between work and play. In both cases these are defined as clearly. Play is articulated as its own purpose whereas both competition and work are externally motivated. The purpose of work lies outside work itself. Competition is by definition an externally defined activity. One is thrown into competition. It represents a condition, which creates a fundamental effort to remain within it and not be ousted. At the same time, the desire for the qualities of play is articulated. It would be desirable for competition to adhere to clear and just rules of the game, for the game board to be visible and for the best people to win and be recognized. It would be desirable for work to function as play and motivation in itself. That would unite happiness and efficiency. The articulation and organization of competitive games take place from the side of the distinctions that emphasizes purpose. That means that we get a re-entry of the distinction competition/play on the competition side, and a re-entry of the distinction work/play on the work side. This can be illustrated as shown in Figure 2.5.

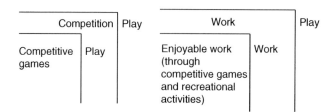

Figure 2.5   Play re-entered as work and competition

Enjoyable work is work that seeks to be play. Competitive games are competition that seeks to be play. The place from which one finds the interest in play is always the place of competition and efficiency. Too much play is identified as a decrease in efficiency and as a demotivating loser mentality. The function of competitive games seems to be that competition as value is at once symbolized, nurtured and disciplined.

2. The semantics of training and simulation games

After World War II and particularly from the mid-1950s, games and organizations become linked in a new and systematic way. Over the course of a few years, there was an explosive growth in the number of articles related to management games and business games. Initially, these games were designed to illustrate simple management principles for example, profit maximization or the relation between price, production costs and profit. From the late 1950s, we see the development of more complicated games aimed at top management in private companies. Subsequently, the games become divided into what is referred to as general management games aimed at top management and functional games aimed at various functions such as marketing, pricing policy, production management, etc. One critic of management games describes the atmosphere among the enthusiasts in the late 1950s: 'At conferences and seminars, thousands of executives willingly are herded together at computer centres; divided into competitive teams; ushered into small, smoke filled rooms equipped with a blackboard and calculating machine; and instructed to spend huge sums of hypothetical money belonging to non-existent enterprises, while a computer keeps score of their executive ability' (Christian 1961: 22).

Figure 2.6 shows the front page of one of the first books about management games.

By the beginning of the 1960s, hundreds of games had been developed and applied in business schools and in in-house training in major companies. The principles for these games had been established, and the development throughout the 1970 and 1980 consisted primarily in further development, in particular in view of the possibilities presented by the accelerating capacity of computers.

Figure 2.6   The first books about management games (from Greene & Sisson 1959)

There is no reference whatsoever to links between play and organizations from before World War II. There are, however, quite a few broad references to so called 'war games', which emerge with World War II. These war games, it is said, were developed as a result of insufficient empirical experiences. The military is not constantly involved in battles and wars where tactics and strategies can be tested, and therefore it has to rely on simulations and war games where theories can be tested without threat to human life. The proponents of management games embrace a similar logic. Even though there are plenty of experiences to draw from in real life, students and young managers can be given the chance to learn about a range of management relations and try out different wild decisions without economic consequences. In 1959, in one of their first books about management games, Jay Greene and Roger Sisson wrote: 'The military has long recognized the value of using simulations for educational purposes. 'War games' for example, are used extensively by the armed forces ... The military has found that games are particularly valuable when it is impossible to participate in the actual situation and also where it would be very expensive to provide on-the-job-experience. Games can be useful in business for the same reasons' (Greene & Sisson 1959: 1). In 1958, G.R. Andlinger wrote about the relation between war games and management games: 'War gaming helps military to: Avoid a historical outlook – the tendency to fight the last war instead of the next. Acquire a healthy respect for the unforeseen, the chance elements, the unplanned. Gain experience in making decisions under pressure and with incomplete information. The parallels to business training appear too clear to require elaboration' (Andlinger 1958b: 151).

Since the 1950s, numerous management games have been developed. Later, I will describe some of the different strategies for their design, but in general they share the following characteristics: The participants are divided into competing teams and are often placed in different rooms. A team represents decision makers in an organization. Sometimes, individual participants are assigned a specific role on the team such as the production or marketing manager. At other times the team merely functions as a management unit. The team represents an organization, and the organization faces an external environment, e.g. a market. The team is presented with data about the external environment and has to make analyses and decisions on the basis of this data. The decisions are entered into a simulation model, sometimes using a computer, and the team is presented with the results of its decisions. These games are repeated a certain number of times. The team who obtains the best economic result wins.

Naturally, there is a broad range of possible variations. One of the best known games, which dates back to 1956 and was further developed throughout the 1960s, is The Carnegie Tech Management Game. When it was introduced in the *Journal of Business* in 1960, the game developers described management games like this: 'Business games, in general, consist in two parts – external environment and internal decisions. The games have usually been built around some given market in which the players making up the several teams compete. The teams or firms are generally required to make such decisions as setting price, determining output, etc. The environment, which is normally programmed on an electronic computer, contains the various functions, such as the demand curve, which determine the outcome for each firm or decisions made. The firms usually receive some form of income statement and balance sheet, and the outcome of their decisions can be traced in the ebb and flow of accounts on the financial statement (Cohen, Cyert, Dill, Kuehn, Miller & Winters 1960: 303).

In addition to the division into general and function-based games, the games can also be divided according to a continuum between mathematical simulation games and empirical games, where the mathematical simulation games are built around a set of general economic laws such as supply and demand. The empirical games, in turn, are constructed around an empirically specific economic field of operation, e.g. a specific line of business, and loaded with correct information about price development, transport routes, wage rates, etc. At one end of the continuum are games such as 'ASA General Management Business Simulation', which is designed to provide the participants with realistic experience in a simulated company with respect to optimal choice of tools and strategic decision-making. The participants have to make decisions about purchasing materials, wages, shipping and storage, pricing, advertisement, market surveys, etc. Another game at the same end of the continuum is 'Burrough Economic Simulator', which focuses in particular on the relation between marketing, investment and production. At the other end of the continuum are games such as 'Air Canada management game', 'Purdue University forest management game' and 'A management game for the petroleum industry', which are all empirically based (Graham & Gray 1969). Figure 2.7 shows an example of a game board from a game from the 1950s.

The game board is described like this: 'Each team has a game board, preferably about 20 by 30 inches, which represents the physical operations of the company. The left-hand half of the game board represents the market, with the tinted areas representing urban markets, the white areas rural markets. Each square is a customer. The right-hand half represents operations; the spaces in the vertical columns

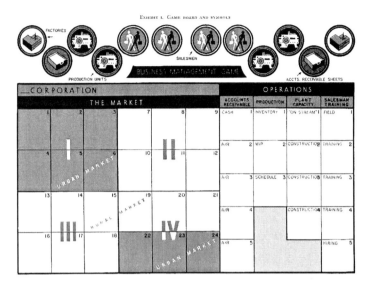

Figure 2.7   Game Board *anno* 1950 (from Andlinger 1958a: 119)

indicate that decisions made during one time period do not become effective until some time in the future. At the beginning of each period all operations move *up* one space' (Andlinger 1958a: 119)

The objective of these games is discussed a lot because the gamers are repeatedly accused of merely playing for fun and the only value of the games being entertainment. We will return to this discussion later. Generally, three general objectives of management games are outlined. The first is education and training of management competencies, the second is analysis and testing of decisions and strategies in companies, and the third is research. Andlinger draws a distinction between problem-solving games and teaching games. He writes about the former: 'A *problem-solving* game is one in which the objective is to arrive at an approximate answer through repeated trials ... A game simulating four competing gasoline stations, for example, might give the players considerable insight into the probable effect of alternative retail pricing strategies' (Andlinger 1958b: 148). About the second kind of games he writes: 'A *teaching game*, on the other hand, has as its main objective the demonstration of already existing insight or principles to participants' (Andlinger 1958b: 148). In general, emphasis is place upon the notion that the individual game should be designed on the basis of clearly formulated objectives. To the extent that the general purpose is education, this should be clarified in the form of management competencies, which it is believed that participants can obtain by playing the game. The Carnegie Tech Management Game emphasizes the following general abilities, which the game is designed to stimulate in participants: (1) the ability to abstract, organize, and use information from a complex and diffuse external environment; (2) the ability to plan and be progressive; (3) the ability to combine the role of the generalist and the specialist; and (4) the ability to work effectively with others (Cohen, Cyert, Dill, Kuehn, Miller & Winters, 1960: 310–311). In addition, in 1964, they incorporate the ability to set goals and define them in an operational manner (Cohen, Cyert, Kuehn & Winters 1964: 9). Director of Western Systems Training Centre, Burt Nanus, contends that good management games: (1) ensure an exceptionally high level of involvement of participants in the learning situation; (2) are much better at demonstrating management principles e.g. statistics and cases studies; (3) demonstrate problems of decision-making; (4) demonstrate the use of management tools; (5) represent effective simulations; and finally (6) the very creation and design process of a game provide excellent insight into company relations (Nanus 1969: 53).

But which specific concept of a game is formed here? Is 'game' merely another name for a management or training tool, or are the concepts of game and play connected and if so, in what way? The relation between game and play is clearly one of the points of contention throughout the 1950s and 1960s. Game is obviously linked to play, but it is also seen as important that games do not become too playful. At the core of the discussions is which qualities of play should not be included in management games. Andlinger says of the relation between management games and play: 'Games are as old as man. Usually their basic objective is entertainment. The business management game, however, aims not at entertainment but at learning. Other differences between it and a game like Monopoly, for example, are: The degree to which it approaches reality and the degree to which the players' experience, judgment and skill – as opposed to luck – influence the outcome. If a business game is to serve a purpose beyond that of a fascinating toy, there must be some transfer of learning from the game situation to reality' (Andlinger 1958a: 117). In a different article, Andlinger makes a distinction between entertaining games such as Monopoly and Poker on one hand and management games on the other. What distinguishes the two types of games is the fact that the purpose of the latter is to teach participants something from reality. However, it is equally interesting to focus on what Andlinger sees as the uniting qualities of entertaining games and management games. Andlinger argues that management games and games of entertainment share conceptual frameworks and types of conflicts. Both types involve conflicts or competition, incomplete information about game rules or about the opponent's strategy, and uncertainty about the result as a consequence of the actions of the opponent or an element of chance. Moreover, Andlinger sees a 'high degree of emotional involvement' as a shared common feature (Andlinger 1958b: 148). Thus Andlinger sees management games as play, but play with a clearly defined learning objective. The conceptual structure of this can be shown as in Figure 2.8.

Accordingly, entertainment games represent clean play whereas management games represent a form of purpose-polluted play, which in turn is accepted as a serious organizational activity.

Paul Greenlaw and Stanford Kight discuss the relation between management games and play from a different perspective under the heading 'Ego involvement: promise or danger?' They acknowledge management games as a form of training that is characterized by a high level of participant involvement as opposed to certain other forms of training, which render participants apathetic. The problem, however, according to them, is that management games lead to *too much* involvement and result in dispute, exaggerated competitiveness and bitter antagonism among players on the individual teams. They

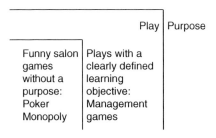

Figure 2.8   Andlinger's concept of management games

argue: 'Gaming sessions are often too highly competitive. Considerable attention is given by the participants to "winning" or "losing", regardless of de-emphasis on the part of the trainer, and a high degree of excitement and anxiety seems to be exhibited by many participants. Considerable over-competitiveness, hostility and defensiveness often prevail within a company group during the decision-making periods. Participants have been known to literally run to meet the umpires with the latest results; they will frequently stay up most of the night after a series of sessions, analysing and reanalysing their data in order to surprise their competitors with a dynamic new strategy the following morning' (Greenlaw & Kight 1960: 58). Greenlaw and Kight simply believe that management games have to be made more boring in order to reduce the level of involvement and increase learning. That can be done, for example by slowing down the speed of the game: 'The pressures and tensions placed upon gaming participants may also be lessened, thereby providing a less threatening situation, by allotting more time for making decisions. Although an overabundance of time will cause boredom and loss of interest among participants, it may well be that much of the potential value is now being lost because too much is being crowded into too short a time, sometimes, for example, decision periods are limited to six or eight minutes' (Greenlaw & Kight 1960: 59). Moreover, Greenlaw and Kight see it as a potential danger that the exaggerated competitive element of the games may displace the human factor. They believe that it is important for participants to develop empathetic skills in relation to interpreting the other teams and the other members of one's own team and to develop sensitivity towards other people's behaviour, attitude, notions and needs. They suggest that an observer is placed on each team so that s/he may present human aspects and data and provide participants with the opportunity to learn about group dynamics after the decision-making period (Greenlaw & Kight 1960: 60–61). Greenlaw and Kight's conceptual structure for the relation between play and game is shown in Figure 2.9.

In the article, 'Don't bet on business games', William Christian assumes a third position, which entirely rejects games as anything but play. Christian writes: 'Even the most complex game models are absurdly simple in comparison with the real world of business [...] The games technique itself will not provide management with a crystal ball. On the other hand, pure simulation, as a long term

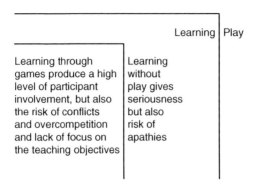

	Learning	Play
Learning through games produce a high level of participant involvement, but also the risk of conflicts and overcompetition and lack of focus on the teaching objectives	Learning without play gives seriousness but also risk of apathies	

Figure 2.9   Greenlaw and Kight's conceptual structure

investment in time, money, and proper personnel, is a good bet for the executive who wants to take a scientific peek into the future of his business. Games are for fun; simulation is for real' (Christian 1961: 66). Simulation is a scientific act. Management games are pure play.

All these operations of distinction between management games and play establish a particular relationship between management games and reality. The games are fundamentally seen as a representation of reality or they would hold no learning purpose. The games are to function as an educational support of participants' acquisition of the roles of decision-makers and managers, and thus their role in the game is required to be realistic in relation to the role they are to assume in the real world of business economics. However, the game is not supposed to be reality or its learning benefits would vanish. Or as Greene and Sisson say of their game: 'Although a Dynamic Management Decision Game does not model any real situation in every detail, it is intended that it has enough of the aspects of reality that the player comes to appreciate the complexities and interrelationships found in an actual business environment' (Greene & Sisson 1959: 3). From the mid-1950s, a distinction between realism and playability is established. One of the designers of McKinsey's game 'The Business Management Game' says: 'We started in 1956 with the idea of applying war-gaming techniques to business. In the course of the year we tested, modified, and retested the game many times to develop a fine balance between realism and playability. The more closely a game resembles reality, the more cumbersome it becomes – until it is no longer playable' (Andlinger 1958a: 117). Carlson and Misshauk also discuss the relationship between game and realism from the perspective of the functionality of the game. Their main point is that: 'Game construction must present enough detail to gain involvement through realism, but should not be so complex as to frustrate the player attempting a rational decision' (Carlson & Misshauk 1972: 3). Carlson and Misshauk observe a conflict of design between realism and simplification, and they generally believe that realism is overemphasized and hurts the game, both as learning and as game. About learning, they say: 'A game model that is too complex does not permit identification of the underlying structural or causal relationship and the impact of the decisions cannot be determined. As a result, learning experience is sublimated into trying to understand, play, and administer a complex game' (Carlson & Misshauk 1972: 13). In relation to the character of the game as a game, the players have to at least feel that they are involved in a meaningful contest with other participants: 'If the participants do not have reasonable control over their destiny through their decisions and are subject to imposed restrictions that take away the feeling of control, the game as a game is likely to be a failure (Carlson & Misshauk 1972: 13). Russel Ackoff (1959) discusses the relation between game and realism from the perspective of realism. He fundamentally supports the use of management games, but believes that the way in which reality is often represented in games is problematic. He believes that simplification and representation can assume different forms, which in different ways affect the functionality of the game. He makes a distinction between two different forms of modelling of reality: Iconic modelling and analogue modelling. Iconic modelling may consist in the contraction of time in the game or the reduction of money. Analogue modelling, on the other hand, consists in the substitution of reality, as when the production of a product is substituted by the production of words, or when actual movements in supply and demand are replaced by a mathematical model. Ackoff prefers analogue models but also points out that the iconic models give the games a sense of realism. However, the biggest problem is the mixing of analogue and iconic models, which makes it impossible to distinguish between iconic and analogue forms of argumentation. That diminishes the scientific nature of the games (Ackoff 1959: 149).

These distinctions between game and reality are based in a specific realistic epistemology. Reality is what it is, and hence it can be represented, formalized, and be included as a realistic premise for the game. Moreover, this reality is considered so stable that it makes sense to also define given roles in relation to their handling of reality; roles that then are to be learned and mastered.

I am going to identify one last theme, namely the relation between game and research. Because these games are generally perceived to be representative models of reality, they are seen as a specific research method. The games are considered a simplified version of reality. Sometimes, reality is so complex that it makes it difficult to conduct research about it. Thus, as a simplified model, the games offer themselves up as a functionally equivalent substitute for reality. In particular, the development of The Carnegie Tech Management Game was connected with a significant level of research ambition. The people behind these games identify five research areas where games can be used as research method: economy; organization; marketing; financing; and production (Cohen, Cyert, Dill, Kuehn, Miller & Winters 1960: 316–321). Games are considered a research tool as a cross between field studies and laboratory experiments (Cohen, Dill, Kuehn & Winters 1964: 272). Games make it possible to study, for example, the way in which 'individuals react to masses of loosely structured information, how they abstract from this information interpretations about state of the environment, and how they formulate problems and define alternatives for decisions' (Cohen, Dill, Kuehn & Winters 1964: 360). In organizational theory, games are considered useful when studying team organization. In which ways are the behaviour and efficiency of a team affected by changes in its size, amount of information, increase of time pressures, etc. (Cohen, Cyert, Dill, Kuehn, Miller & Winters 1960: 317–320)? There are actual examples from the period of published researched articles that are based on games, e.g. Herman Hutte's study of decision-making in management games (Hutte 1965).

The semantics surrounding management games evolved between 1955 and 1970 and then the debate about management games and their potential subsided. However, the development of management games has not. To this day, new games are under continual development, and it seems as if they are occasionally rediscovered, as demonstrated by the journal *Training and Development* printing of

Figure 2.10   The Virtual Leader (*Associate managment* 2001, Virtual Leader Business Skills Suit, http://www.simulearn.net/leadershiptraining/leadership_simulations.html)

an article in 1991 with the title 'Simulations: Learning tools for the 1990s'. The article recognizes the fact that simulation games are not an entirely new phenomenon, but it argues that in the 1990s, all previously formulated visions will be able to be fulfilled: 'In the 1990s, simulations may finally fulfil their promise. Advances in computer and media-based technologies – and in our understanding of decision theory, organizational behaviour, and organizational learning – have opened the door for more widespread use of simulations' (McAteer 1991: 19). New board games are developed, such as Zodiak in 2001 and CD-Rom games such as Virtual Leader (see Figure 2.10), which was released in 2003 and which can be played on a personal computer (*Associate Management* 2001, Virtual Leader Business Skills Suit, http://www.simulearn.net/leadershiptraining/leadership_simulations.html).

Summary

From the mid-1950s, a number of training and simulation games emerged for use in large companies, business schools, etc. The games became engulfed in an independent semantics with a differentiated discussion of relations between games, management and learning. Unlike the preceding period, the games did not merely function as representations of characteristics of the reality of companies and other organizations. The games were given an independent function, particularly with respect to the training of roles of decision-making and management in companies. The games are associated with play and are perceived as a way to involve participants in learning processes through which participants assume predefined roles as decision maker, company strategy, investor, personnel manager, etc. The element of play should not be allowed to be too dominant but should be linked to unambiguous organizational objectives. The relation between the game and an organizational reality consists of the requirement for the game to function as a simplified representation of such a reality.

3. The semantics of making the world appear through play

The first indications of the emergence of a new semantics about the relationship between organization and play can be seen at the beginning of the 1980s. At staff training and management courses, seminars and conferences about organizational development, personnel issues, strategy and change processes, social games become included as a conscious effort to support creative and educational processes. The common name for these is 'icebreakers'. One example from 1983 is Sue Forbess-Greene's book *The Encyclopedia of Icebreakers*. Forbess-Greene sees the so-called icebreakers as games that are designed to facilitate learning for participants in workshops, courses, conferences, etc. Icebreakers are tools designed to help course directors and others create interaction, stimulate creative thinking, and illustrate new concepts (Forbess-Greene 1983: 1). Forbess-Greene distinguishes between six different types of icebreakers, each with their specific core functions. These are: (1) Energizers and tension reducers; (2) Feedback and disclosure; (3) Games and brainteasers; (4) Getting acquainted; (5) Openers and warm-ups; and (6) Professional development topics (Forbess-Greene 1983: 4). As an example, the first type of icebreaker is designed to reduce the level of tension and anxiety in a given group and energize the participants in a situation which might otherwise be felt as stressful (Forbess- Greene 1983: 7). An example of a specific icebreaker is 'Barnyard' and is aimed at a group of players who know each other but where the relationship is still characterized by internal tension and mutual uncertainty. In this game, the players have to use animal sounds to recognize one another. One player volunteers to play the role of the farmer. The remainder of the players plays the role of farm animals. The farmer is blindfolded and is spun around. The other players are placed around him. Now, the farmer must call the animals, e.g. by saying 'cow'. The player who is closest to the farmer then has to respond by saying 'moo'. The farmer now has to recognize the players by their animal sounds. Once a player has been recognized, he or she has to take the role of the farmer. The game ends when each player has played the role of farmer (Forbess-Greene 1983: 9). Clearly, the relationship between organization and play is defined in radically different terms than in the preceding phase. The use of play is much more pure, and the connection between play and childishness is explicitly articulated in positive terms. We will return to a discussion of this later.

The concept of icebreakers marked the beginning of a new notion of play from the beginning of the 1980s, and by the 1990s the entire field was swamped by new types of games and play aimed at almost any aspect of the organizational sphere, e.g. team building, quality management, diversity, self-esteem, and team performance. The games are no longer only used at special occasions such as workshops and courses but are included in the organizational routine as a fixed part of day to day management. As can be seen in the above-mentioned example, these games are of an entirely different character. Only rarely are they very factually complex and lengthy games supported by computers and other mathematical equipment. Most of these games are described in one to five pages, emphasize social relations, and usually last only about half an hour. Thus, their semantics are often expressed in a very different way, that is, as reference books comprising of between 20 and 100 games. These are big books with tiles such as *Icebreakers – A sourcebook of games, exercises and simulations, The wrecking yard of games and activities, Quality games for trainers, 60 role plays for management and supervisory training, The fun factor, 104 activities that build, The big book of team building games, The complete games trainers play, Leadership games, Beyond boredom and anxiety, Games that teach teams, 50 creative training openers & energizers, Fun and gains. Motivate and energize staff with workplace games, contest and activities,*

103 additional training games, and *Thiagis 100 favourite games*. These books are usually given colourful covers with drawings of adult participants engaged in play. The cover of *103 additional training games* is an illustration of a game in which a woman, using verbal instructions, is trying to help a blindfolded man navigate his way from one island drawn on the floor to another. These islands are inscribed with game signs taken from the principles inside the book. Often the book illustrations and drawings are characterized by a somewhat childish pen. Some of the books use either child-like or creative typography. In general, they are characterized by the effort not to appear boring. A few of the books draw on the personal authority of its author, typically on the back of the books. The book *Thiagis 100 favourite games* even carries a large photograph of the author on the front cover. On the back cover we are told that the author holds a PhD, that he has published 40 books and more than 200 articles, designed 120 games, been an international consultant, lived in three different countries, given hundreds of presentations around the world, and been a keynote speaker at countless professional conferences. Moreover, the book begins with a short chapter about the author himself and his life story. Although this book might be extreme, these books generally draw on the personal reputation of the author. The games seem to be supported by their personal authority and personal experiences and testing of the games (or sometimes, reference is made to friends of the authors as the origin of a game and certain experiences).

Whereas, in the preceding phase, play was not to be exaggerated and was meant primarily to function as an attraction, there are no reservations about play and playfulness in this next phase. As mentioned previously, the characteristics of play are obvious in the design of the books. There are, however, certain disagreements as to how much fun should be involved. The majority of game books are based on the notion that play has to take place in a purposeful way and that play and games represent a necessary method for fulfilling the objectives in question because play is seen as a way to establish social relations and as a method for collective learning. Marlene Caroseli, the author of the book *Quality games for trainers* writes: 'Each game begins with a statement of the objective. Although we call these activities games they are not all fun and games. They are enjoyable work – not mindless busywork [. . .] Usually some kind of competition is involved along with a lighthearted focus' (Caroseli 1996: xiii). John Newstrom and

Edward Scannel write with a similar perspective on game and fun: In short, games help team members have *fun* while learning a key point. Don't use games just to entertain. High-performance teams want to be productive and use their time wisely; don't waste valuable meeting time by using a game solely to entertain (Newstrom & Scannell 1998: xxvii). Play is serious business but is not defined in opposition to play.

There are, however, some game designers for whom fun is an objective in itself. Fun is serious business and, to some, constitutes the whole philosophy behind the game designs. One such designer is Carolyn Greenwich, author of *The fun factor* and *Fun and gains*, who motivates and energizes staff with workplace games, contests and activities. Greenwich argues that fun is an important element in the workplace. 'People learn and achieve more when the process is enjoyable. Fun activities motivate and energize and make results easier to achieve for all' (Greenwich 2000: viii). She goes on: 'The fun activities are designed mainly to boost the morale and generate a positive atmosphere in the office. All managers agree that when their staff are feeling happy, they give better customer service, generate more sales, and are more productive at work' (Greenwich 1997: viii). Play and games are used to create a positive atmosphere in which people feel that they are having fun while working.

Alanna Jones does indeed celebrate play and fun but from an entirely different perspective. Her point is not that games and fun in the sales office ensure success and a competitive team spirit. Her standpoint is therapeutic and she considers play a positive form of existence and a resource for personal development. Her book, *104 activities that build* even begins with a preamble celebrating games, play and fun: 'To my son Corbin who continually shows me the joy that comes from games and play and who makes the game of life more fun to live!' (Jones 1998). And in the preface to the book it says: 'The games in this book are designed to be fun and interactive ... So, have fun, be safe, know the limits of the members of your group, and always give people the choice of participation to ensure a good time for all!' (Jones 1998). Alanna Jones places independent therapeutic value on game and play. It is fine that games can be assigned a therapeutic objective, but in addition, games and play have an immanent positive therapeutic effect: 'Games have a therapeutic value in themselves – the reason people who are depressed are encouraged to engage in activities and why people at a fair or carnival are smiling and having a good time.

Families are encouraged to build better relationships with each other by playing together and by participating in games that are enjoyable and fun for all. Think about your own life and the things that you do that are fun and enjoyable. How do the activities make you feel and how do they help you in your daily life? The answer to this question should be that the fun games you play and activities that you enjoy help you feel better, both emotionally and physically ... Games get you involved with other people, build relationships among individuals, make everyone equal and most of all promote laughter to help people have a good time' (Jones 1998: 11–12).

In the preceding phase, one often spoke of games but rarely explicitly about play. Games were an adult activity, which could be given an objective. Play was marked as a purposeless children's activity. In this phase, a number of game designers sought to abolish this distinction, partly because a number of games were designed to be played by children, young people, and adults alike. That pertains, for example, to Alanna Jones book *The wrecking yard of games and activities*. The themes she deals with such as communication, self-esteem and cooperation, are not defined by specific age groups. She believes, therefore, that her games have relevance in the workplace, in schools, in hospitals, etc. (Jones 1996). Furthermore, Alanna Jones considers childhood as such a fundamental source of inspiration for further development of games. Because she sees games and play as holding immanent and independent therapeutic value, she also believes that professional therapists are able to bring out and develop this value: 'When thinking of games, think of what you played as a child or even games you play now, and often times these games can be adopted to create a new therapeutic game by changing the game slightly or adding a discussion, and before you know it you will have a new game that focuses on specific goals, objectives, and issues' (Jones 1998: 14). In conclusion, Alanna Jones reminds her readers: 'Don't forget to have fun, laugh and enjoy yourself while in the process of helping others learn more about themselves and the world around them' (Jones 1998: 17).

The difference that is repeatedly used can be formalized as shown in Figure 2.11.

The distinction between play and serious business is used again and again, however, as soon as the distinction has been made, it is re-entered into itself on the side of play as play with what is serious. And in Newstrom and Scannell, fun is a serious matter, which means

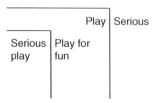

Figure 2.11   Serious play

that playing for the purpose of having fun means to play with what is serious.

Not everyone agrees with Alanna Jones. Ken Jones appreciates fun games, but he defines a limit that applies to games, which, as he says, are merely silly or childish, psychotherapeutic or invade ones private life: 'In contrast to many other icebreakers, I tried to avoid the trivial and childish. I left out party games. There is no fanning a balloon across a chalk line, no catching a plate before it stops spinning, nor are there psycho-therapeutic events. Participants are not asked to reveal the innermost feelings. Missing are all those activities where a person stands in the middle of a group and falls only to be pushed upright again by supportive members. Also are missing the dramatic role-plays in which people have to playact – something which many find difficult and some may regard as an invasion of their privacy. Such events can be icemakers rather than icebreakers' (Jones 1994: 12). He goes on to explain: 'This book does not treat the participants as patients, or actors or children' (Jones 1994: 12). Nevertheless, games are not prohibited from being fun and playful: 'I have tried to provide plenty of scope for mind jogging, for humour, for amusing initiatives. I hope this book will provoke events that can be appreciated and enjoyed on an adult level' (Jones 1994: 12).

In many of these books the words play, simulation, activity, exercises, game, training, and role-play are used almost interchangeably. Only rarely are clear distinctions made between them. For example, for John Newstrom and Edward Scannell, game simply functions as a joint term for activities, exercises, and icebreakers that make meeting more fun by opening up feelings and lifting the spirits of the team members (Newstrom & Scannell 1998: xiv). Sivasailam Thiagarajan only makes a distinction between games and activities. Activities are defined rather openly as events, including training events that a person participates in. According to this definition all games are therefore simultaneously an activity but not the other way around (Thiagarajan 2006: 2). There are very clear minimum criteria for how an activity can also be said to be a game. A game is defined by its adherence to four characteristics: 'conflict, control, closure, and contrivance' (Thiagarajan 2006: 2). '*Conflict* arises when players have a goal. Conflict frequently occurs in the form of competition among players or teams. But you can also have cooperative games in which the conflict is represented by previous records, tight time limits, and limits of resources' (Thiagarajan 2006: 2). Control refers to the rules of the game. Closure refers to the specific rule that determines when the game is over. The final variable is contrivance: '*Contrivance* refers to the characteristics of a game that makes people say, After all, it was only a game. This term refers to the built-in inefficiencies in a game' (Thiagarajan 2006: 2). This latter quality stresses the fact that the game is play and thus provides participants with the possibility to distance themselves from the game and its result.

Gary Kroehnert makes a distinction between play (games), simulations, brain teasers, role-plays and case studies. He explains these distinctions by saying that they are broad and probably could be defined differently and that experienced supervisors are encouraged to use their own definitions. Game is defined in this way: 'A game is an exercise where participants are involved in a contest with someone else (or a group of people) with a set of rules imposed. Games normally include some type of pay-off' (Kroehnert 2001: 4). Simulations: 'A simulation is a mock-up of an actual or imaginary situation. Simulations are generally used to train future operators where it's impractical or dangerous for these trainees to use real-life equipment or locations. Simulations are normally designed to be as realistic as possible so that trainees can learn from their actions without the financial worries of repairing or replacing damaged equipment (Kroehnert 2001: 4)'. Brain teasers: 'Brain teasers are in a class of their own. They are neither pure games nor simulations but puzzles that either keep participants minds busy or highlight keypoints' (Kroehnert 2001: 4). Role-plays: 'Role-plays are used in training to see how participants react in certain situations before and after training sessions . . . Even when participants do it wrong, they still learn' (Kroehnert 2001: 4). Case studies: 'Case studies are exactly what the name implies' (Kroehnert 2001: 4). Gary

Kroehnert does not explicitly define a criterion for making such distinctions except by saying that these are distinctions that are practical to him. Thus, he may implicitly take a didactic perspective according to which games, exercises, etc. are seen as comparable educational techniques. Therefore, his concept of games is directed more towards a statement about the educational evidence of games than towards a statement about games as games.

In this context, Ken Jones probably provides us with the most reflective concept of distinction. Jones makes a distinction between games, exercises, and simulations, and he takes these distinctions very seriously. He says: 'Some authors have argued that since everybody uses the labels interchangeably the usage does not matter and that to look at meanings is just a dry semantic debate about definitions'. Maybe, but definitions do not become tearful and call each other sons of bitches. Icebreakers are about people: people can be hurt and they matter ... In this book the categorizing of events by methodology is an attempt to minimize or avoid unnecessary unpleasantness, inefficiency and muddle' (Jones 1994: 14). Jones does not establish his distinction between games, exercises and simulations on the basis of their inherent materiality or independent form but on the basis of how they are viewed and played by participants and facilitator. The central question in any interactive learning activity is the way in which the participants treat this activity. The same interactive learning activities can be treated *as if* they are a game, in which the participants represent players who are dutifully obliged to try to win. The same activities can also be approached as if they were an exercise that handles problems and riddles, or they can be treated as if they were a simulation involving professional roles and functions (Jones 1994: 14). It can lead to trouble if the same activities are approached differently by different participants, e.g. if some are focused on winning while others are focused on problem solving. Ken Jones asserts: 'Games, exercises and simulations are not only different from each other, they are incompatible. If some people treat an event as a game while others behave as if it were an exercise or simulation then the result will be disappointing, or unpleasant, or even disastrous. It is important to know what methodology you are supposed to be in' (Jones 1994: 33). From this perspective, game is a methodology with mechanisms that allow us to identify a winner and rules that need no external justifications. One cannot play Monopoly and then suddenly begin to argue the fairness of rent levels, in the same way that it does not make sense in a game logic to accuse Monopoly of not being *like* the real world. In a game methodology, there is only one role for the participants to play, that is, the role of player, which is about trying to win within the boundaries of the given rules. Within a methodology of exercises, there are no rules except for those defined by decision makers or problem-solvers. In an exercise one can say, 'I have solved the problem, but not, I have won or I have lost' (Jones 1994: 33). And finally in a methodology of simulation where it is the environment that is being simulated, there are no dramas and the participants are not actors who identify with their roles and take them on as personalities. Simulations assign functions or duties to participants such as journalist or manager, but the methodology does not allow for participants to pretend that they are in fact, deep down, journalists. They are merely to fill out their function, e.g. write stories or make decisions based on the intention to act professionally (Jones 1994: 33).

As we have already mentioned, there are countless books about organizational and management games each of which contain a large number of different games. All in all, I have probably studied a few thousand games, and despite the fact that some of them are rather similar, there is still a great deal of heterogeneity. However, even in this heterogeneity different regularities seem to emerge. I refer, loosely based on Foulcaultian concepts, to these regularities as strategies of play and games (Foucault 1986, Andersen 1997: 22). What I mean by strategies of play and games is a delimited meaningful regularity of irregular games and play. Each strategy comprises of a level of agreement about reasons for engaging in play and games. There is a certain teleology of playing. At the same time, there is within a strategy also meaningful competition and disagreement about which games most effectively achieves the general purpose. There is not, however, agreement among the strategies as to the objective of the activity of designing games but only agreement about the validity of designing games for organizations. What characterizes relations between strategies is incompatibility with respect to what can and should be achieved through organizational games, what issues can be breached, which rules apply to acceptability and the design of new games, and activities.

Below I make a distinction between six different strategies of play and games. Together, they cover many of the games I have studied, but I do not consider this a complete description of existing strategies. There are so many books and games within this field, and despite the fact that I have aimed to broadly and comprehensively collect the material, I am almost certain that the existing material exceeds my selection. The task is further complicated by the fact that many of the strategies share common themes, which are, however, observed from different positions.

I have already briefly mentioned the icebreaker strategy. As Ken Jones notes metaphorically, 'it is a question of clearing passages in frozen water and opening up the channels of communication' (Jones 1994: 11). The icebreaker strategy is employed in particular in training courses and seminars where the atmosphere is somewhat tense because the participants do not know each other or in an effort to re-energize the group after hours of discussions. But icebreakers are also designed to be used in workplaces with established tension between colleagues or where tension has developed in connection with new projects or tasks whose introduction has created anxiety. Barnyard is an icebreaker. Another is autobiography. The participants fill out a questionnaire with approximately 15 to 20 questions regarding their place of birth, favourite movie, favourite book, number of children, etc, which they then hand over to the seminar leader. Everyone is then given a new questionnaire in which a few of the questions have been answered in advance. The task is then for the participants to circulate among each other to find the person who has given a particular answer, e.g that *The Satanical Verses* is their favourite book. Games break the ice and establish networks between people (Pike & Solem 2000: 11). A third strategy is called *Dreams and Nightmares*. This game is introduced at the beginning of the seminar. The participants are each given a dream card and a nightmare card. On the dream card, participants write down positive expectations of the seminar and negative expectations on the nightmare card. Then, dreams and nightmares are exchanged in groups of participants. At the end, the cards are collected and are posted on a nightmare board and a dream board (Pike & Solem 2000: 28–29).

One can find countless sites on the Internet about such games. Figure 2.12 is a photo of game participants involved in an icebreaker game called *A Puzzling Team*, which is designed towards the opening of a workshop or a meeting.

Table 2.2   Strategies of play and games

Strategies	Themes	Games	Telos

Icebreaker	Network building
	Responsibility
	  tensions
	Relational tensions
	Personal tensions
	Openings
	Energy
	Warming-up
	Creative thinking
		Barnyard
		Trust me
		Whom do you trust?
		Autobiographical
		  sheets
		Who am I like?
		Motivators
		Dreams and
		  nightmares
			Breaking the ice in
			communication
			where channels of
			communication have
			become tense

Therapy	Self-esteem
	Group work
	Self-recognition
	Communication
	Anger management
	Teamwork
	Emotional
	  communication
	Sharing emotions
	Identity
	Stories
	Positive attitude
	Personal future
	  and goals
		Possible predictions
		Emotion bench
		Emotion in motion
		Newspaper about me
		Your time
		How I see you, how
		  you see me
			Building confidence,
			self-esteem, identity,
			cooperation,
			mutuality, and
			communication

TQM	Customer satisfaction
	Value increase
	Empowerment
	Management
	Team management
	Project selection
	Continued learning
	Improved meeting
	  processes
	Paradigm shift
	Role shift
	Benchmarking
	Internal partnerships
	External partnerships
		Quality council
		Esprit de Corps
		Removing barriers
		Quality in/Quality out
		Complain and explain
		Circle of power
		Value the value-added
		A question of learning
		Volunteering
		Meeting assessment
		Think the unthinkable
		The fear factor
		From real to ideal to
		  real again
			Building an
			organization capable
			of continual
			improvement
			through systematic
			data-based learning

Fun and attitude	Attitudes Competition Awards and prizes Motivation Celebrations Happenings Holidays Dressing up Exchange of jokes Top performances	Motivator of the week The birthday Zone The gossip columnist Sales World cup People say the darnedest things The turkey award The mad month Slave for the day Staff appreciation day	Creating the right atmosphere in which employees can have fun, where performance is strong, and where employees attain a winning attitude

(Continued)

Table 2.2   Continued

Strategies	Themes	Games	Telos
	Building courage and morale Personal certificates Appreciation		
Team building	Team building Facilitation Team spirit Shared management Group Virtual teams Mutual responsibility Agreement Mutual understanding Management of disagreement Handling opposition Team learning Trust Goal articulation Planning Vision, mission, identity	So much in common Team discovery What's our name? Logo? Slogan? Most? Best? Greatest? Team building What's the problem? Goal setting/action plan The human spider web Managing chance Duel identity Name that team Cross-roads	Re-organizing a group of loosely connected team members into a productive and dynamic team capable of self-management, of establishing its own goals and strategies, and shape its own identity and mutual responsibility
Change management	Diversity Innovation Conflict management Cooperation Engagement Organizational change Evaluation Learning Self-management Communication Problem solving	Innovation mace Shaping the future Ritual conflict Diversity bingo Mapping diversity Team profile Problem-solving cycle	Developing and changing the organization by using and developing its human resources and by creating learning environments

The *Therapy strategy* is about developing self-esteem, confidence, identity, cooperation, mutuality and communication. Alanna Jones refers to it as a question of helping individuals who feel at an impasse with respect to recharging their lives and helping them to grow emotionally into better people (Jones 1998: 11). According to Alanna Jones, people are filled with good and bad memories and experiences. Negative experiences and negative comments from others often stick longer and more deeply than good experiences, the negative

Figure 2.12 A puzzling team (http://www.teambuilding123.com/?gclid= CNfhksij5YoCFQvilAodekVHyA)

experiences may lead to low self-esteem. Society prohibits adults in particular from praising and commending themselves, which is why adults depend on other adults to commend and appreciate them. Many of the games are designed in a way so that participants are complimented and get to hear positive things about themselves (Jones 1998: 75–76). They learn to give and receive compliments, which are seen as important lessons in order to improve cooperation with others. One of the exercises is called 'How do you see me, how do I see you'. The participants are divided into groups, in which everyone is assigned a partner. Everyone then has to define one thing that symbolizes themselves and one thing that symbolizes their partner, e.g. a flower, a stone, a branch, or something entirely different. Subsequently, the group gets together and presents and shares their symbols. When one participant presents the symbol for the partner to the partner, they explain the symbol and the partner may then ask questions about the symbol and express his or her agreement or disagreement. Together with the partner, the participant then discusses whether the symbol adequately represents the partner or themselves, whether it was easier to come up with a symbol for the partner or for themselves, whether the symbol arrived at by the partner came as a

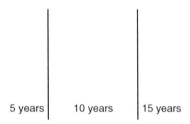

Figure 2.13 Possible predictions

surprise, etc. (Jones 1996: 106–107). Another game is called 'Possible predictions'. The introduction to this game says: 'Knowing what you want in your life and striving to get there keeps you motivated, as the more you work towards your goals the more likely you are to reach them. People who don't have goals or who can't picture themselves doing anything positive with their lives often end up right where they expected and they fell unhappy and unfulfilled. Getting people to think about their future is an important step towards creating a good one' (Jones 1998: 164). The participants are given a piece of paper divided into 5, 10, and 15 years as shown in Figure 2.13. One person writes his or her name on the paper and passes it on to the person next to them, who then has to write down his or her predictions about that person's life in 5, 10, and 15 years. Then the paper is folded over and passed on to the next person who makes his or her predictions without knowing those of the previous person. The predictions have to be positive and reflect positive characteristics of the person in question. At the end, each person is given a piece of paper containing the predictions of all the other participants, so that each person is offered a multiplicity of positive predictions about his or her future. The game concludes with a discussion of whether one would have made similar predictions about oneself, whether some of the predictions came as a surprise, and the possibility of perhaps seeking to realize any of the predictions (Jones 1998: 164–165).

The *TQM strategy* (Totality Quality Management) is about building organizations capable of continually improving themselves through systematic data-based learning. TQM is a movement that dates back to the 1920s in America and is, in fact, not at all about games. However, the game books that do write themselves into the TQM tradition distinguish between its hard and soft sides. TQM is best well known for its hard sides. These are about quantitatively documented organizational development processes. The soft sides, on the other hand, are described as concerning TQM's human relations such as team building, empowerment, leadership, and user satisfaction. It is in relation to these softer categories that games are considered to have a viable function for TQM. Games are thought to be able to support and illustrate TQM's Human Resources principles. These include the principle of benchmarking activities on several levels: on the level of individual, team and organization. Another principle is that there is always room for improvement on all levels. A third principle speaks to the notion that the people closest to a particular process usually have the most insight into them and hence need to be empowered to make all decisions concerning the processes in question (Caroselli 1996: 2). There are several other principles but these will suffice to give a general sense of the TQM logic. There are a number of clear principles, and all the games within this strategy are linked rather explicitly to these principles. The TQM strategy emphasizes the fact that games are fun and it is important to keep employees interested, but at the same time they are not introduced as games. There are often serious questions of reflection tied to the games. One example is called 'The process owner as decision-maker' and refers back to the principle of empowerment. The game is designed to last 20 minutes and is meant to illustrate the concept that a decision has to be made on the lowest level possible. The participants are divided into groups of two. An overhead introduces one question at a time, which the participants then have to discuss. They are given a few minutes for each question. Some of the questions are: (1) How long have you been doing this particular job? What have you learned about it? (2) To what extent do you make decisions concerning it? (3) What was the last thing you did to improve the output of one process related to the job? (4) What other ideas do you have for improving processes (Caroselli 1996: 13). In the end, participants are asked who of them are willing to approach their managers in order to obtain more possibilities for making decisions. Another empowerment game is called 'Circle of power' in which the participants draw three circles on a piece of paper. The first circles is called M and represents the participant in the organization. The next circle is called B and represents the participant's manager (Boss). The last one is called O and represents the organization. More than likely, these circles have different sizes

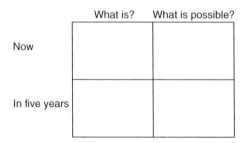

Figure 2.14   The Win/Wip model (from Caroselli 1996: 263)

and are meant to initiate reflections and discussion about the way in which one sees the relationship between the three entities (Caroselli 1996: 75). A third game is called 'From real to ideal to real again'. The point of departure for this game is the notion in TMQ of seeing the possible in the impossible, which is created over time and becomes visible to others in the organization. The participants are asked to fill in the Win/Wip model shown in Figure 2.14. They are then divided into groups where they are told to show each other their models and discuss questions such as; What is your organizations vision for the future?, What is the vision among members of your work unit for the work unit in 5 years?, Which things were not possible to see 5 years ago which it is possible to see in your workplace today?, and What would it take for you to move you work unit from what it is now to what is possible? (Caroselli 1996: 263).

The 'fun and attitude' strategy is basically about creating a productive atmosphere in the workplace. Building a workplace in which everyone has fun is seen as an independent objective. David Abramis asserts that all managers should define goals for how much fun they and their employees should have. He notes: 'Job satisfaction is certainly important. But fun is just as essential to productivity and often harder to find' (Abramis 1989: 36). In this strategy, humour is an independent goal. Eric Romero, professor of management, argues in a study that humour has a positive impact on the work of individuals and groups: Humour is more than a source of amusement. It provides valuable outcomes for teams and organizations (Romero 2005: 146). Moreover, it is a question of developing the right attitude towards work. Preferably, this combines a winning attitude with having a good and fun time. Carolyn Greenwich says it this way: 'It all starts with your attitude. You can never have a bad day if you have a good attitude. A manager's job is to create and maintain winning attitudes and not allow apathy and negativity to creep into the workplace' (Greenwich 2000: 1). Games, fun, laughter and humour are here seen as central and are observed as tools for creating empowerment. In an article in the journal *Empowerment in Organizations*, Jacqueline Miller writes: 'The lack of joy, celebration and humour destroy a feeling of self-worth and self-empowerment'. Motivation is destroyed in organizations that do not provide an empowering environment (Miller 1996: 17). The solution is more fun and games: 'During playing (working) together it becomes evident that fun at work has a genuine and positive effect on creativity and productivity. Employees tap their inner child who has an unquenchable belief that we can do anything in the whole world that we desire to do' (Miller 1996: 17). 'Humour is indeed a powerful tool and can bring about much benefit for the company ... Joyful coolers, cartoons, jokes, toys, games, and music can help people to reactivate all intelligence centres of the brain. Getting back to the inner child can greatly help to put more joy into life, and especially into work' (Miller 1996: 255). Game designers within this strategy see themselves, among other things, as humour consultants (Miller 1996: 17). One example of a game is 'Slave for the day', which rewards the employee with play money over a 3-month period for certain responsibilities, e.g. punctuality, fulfilment of certain tasks, or tidying up the work station. After 3 months, the workplace organizes an auction, and the employee who makes the highest bid wins the right to hold his or her manager as slave for a day, and as the game description says: what could be more fun than bossing the boss (Greenwich 1997: 20–21). According to the game concept, this type of game brings managers closer to the employees and creates fun in the workplace. Other games are more simply designed to create social events, where employees have a good time with each other. These include 'Morning of new arrivals', 'Potluck lunch', and 'Christmas lunch', where the employees children are welcome (Greenwich 1997: 4–8). Another game is called *Holy Cows*. The purpose of this game is to get rid of outmoded and ineffective procedures and routines. The game takes on the character of a campaign, which may run for several months. Pictures of cows are posted on the walls around the workplace. Small plastic cows are placed on desks and other surfaces. Paper cows are hung from the ceiling. Employees are encouraged to point out 'holy cows' to the management, bring new ideas to the table, and suggest rules they believe should be abolished, and if their ideas become reality, the employee in question is awarded a cow certificate which is hung in a public place (Greenwich 2000: 64–68).

The *Teambuilding strategy* is about reconfiguring a group of loosely connected team members into a productive and dynamic team, capable of self-management, creating own goals and strategies, and establishing its own identity and mutual responsibility. The teambuilding strategy works from the concept that a team cannot be built by anyone outside the team. Referring to a group of employees as a team does not make a team, since a team does not become a team until it creates itself as a team. Steve Sugar and George Takacs defines the question of team or no team as a continuum with the classification team spirit on the lowest level of the hierarchy, where a team is only a team to the extent that there is a group of people who like working together but where there is no shared responsibility and no self-management. On the other end of the continuum is what they refer to as a cutting edge model, which is a self-managing team with shared leadership, shared responsibility, shared goals, and a mutually effective style (Sugar & Takacs 2000: 3–6). The goal becomes to help a team move from one end of the continuum to the other. That is teambuilding. Hence, the games within this strategy focus on guiding the team manager towards making the teams create themselves, and the different games typically focus on different elements of this self-creation. Newstrom and Scannell makes a distinction between stages of teambuilding. The game is intended to help create the conditions of interactions, which allow a team to develop (Newstrom & Scannell 1998: xi–xvi). Newstrom and Scannell believe that at different stages of a teambuilding process, different questions arise. Their game is designed to help the team to tackle these questions. They distinguish between 13 general questions according to which the games differentiate themselves. Together, these questions are termed key questions in formations. The questions taken from Newstrom & Scannell (1998: xvii–xxii) are:

1. Who are they?
2. Who are we?
3. Why should we be a team?
4. What if we aren't all alike?
5. Whom do we trust?

6. Where are we headed and what is our route?
7. How are we doing?
8. How can we do things differently?
9. Can we get along better?
10. How can we work together/better?
11. What lies ahead?
12. How can we have more fun?
13. How can we reinforce each other?

Question six, for example, concerns goals and norms for the team but also the function and mission underlying the goals and their implementation. Games for this question focus on making the team define what is acceptable and worth pursuing and what is unacceptable and dysfunctional. 'What's the problem?' is a way to play ones way to the meeting agenda so that it is the team who defines the problems to be worked on (Newstrom & Scannell 1998: 91). As a follow-up to this, 'Best and Worst' is a game designed to support the formation and definition of team norms and introduce complex issues in a pleasant way. The team members are encouraged to yell out what they find to be the worst and the best about a particular issue concerning the team. This could be team cooperation, meeting culture, or something else. Then a best and a worst list are posted on the wall. During the meeting, the members of the team are interviewed about the different points and the meeting concludes with a discussion of how to support the best and avoid the worst (Newstrom & Scannell 1998: 89–90). The game 'So much in common' seeks to demonstrate that people have more in common than they think and is about creating shared team identity. A preprinted piece of paper (see Figure 2.15) is distributed among participants, who are asked to get together in groups of two.

Name:	Name:	Name:
1.	1.	1.
2.	2.	2.
3.	3.	3.
4.	4.	4.
...	...	...

Figure 2.15 So much in common (from Newstrom & Scannell 1998: 25)

The purpose of their conversation is to locate things the two have in common. The participants write down things they have in common with their conversation partner. This conversation lasts two to three minutes. Then the participants change conversation partners and the procedure is repeated a few times. The came ends with a shared discussion with the following guiding questions: (1) How many of you found more than 15 things in common? (2) What were some of the unusual items you discovered? (3) How did you uncover these areas of commonality? (4) Is it likely that in most situations we may well find similar results, i.e. we have much more in common than we otherwise might think? (5) What implications does this have for us as members of a team or of a diverse workforce? (Newstrom & Scannell 1998: 25).

The last strategy, *change management*, is concerned with developing and changing the organization by making use of and developing human resources and by creating learning environments. Play has for long time been observed as a central issue regarding organizational learning within sociology of organizations (March & Olsen 1976, March 1981, March & Levitt 1988). However, it is more recently that we can observe an explosion in designs of specific change and innovations games. Among its themes are innovation, change processes, employee development and conflict mediation. A major group of games within this strategy focus on diversity and multiplicity in the workplace. If an organization and its employees do not have an eye for its diversity, they overlook human resources that could potentially be beneficial to the organization. Therefore, these games seek to locate multiplicity and diversity on the basis of given categories such as gender and ethnicity. However, many of the games are about establishing multiple categories of diversity. One of these games is called 'Diversity bingo' the objective of which is described this way: 'Diversity bingo invites participants to understand the extent to which they themselves stereotype others solely on the basis of superficial characteristics. It also introduces members of a group to the dimensions of diversity that exist within the group' (Kaagan 1999: 146). The first part of the game is the making of the board for the game and its diversity categories. The board might look like the one shown in Figure 2.16.

Another diversity game is called 'Differences' and is described in this way: I am always amazed and confused about the fact that we are all different in so many different ways. I use 'Differences' to provoke people into realizing that diversity goes beyond just racial or

Diversity Bingo Card

Person who has served meals in a soup kitchen.	Person who has milked a cow.	Person who knows how to do regression analysis.	Person who has more than one set of step-siblings or stepchildren.	Person who has attended a "Take Back the Night" rally.
Person who has overcome a disability.	A single parent.	Person who shared a home meal with a family of a different race.	Person who has lived more than 5 years in a town of less than 2,000.	Person who is first college grad in his or her nuclear family.
Person who knows someone who uses food stamps.	Person who has prayed at a mosque.	Person who speaks two or more languages.	Person who has done bungi jumping.	Person who has played a wheelchair sport.
Person born in an Asian country.	Person who has dated someone of a different race.	A single child.	Male with paid child care experience.	Person who has run for political office.
Person who rode a city bus to and from work or school.	Female who has worked on a construction crew.	Person who has lived in another country for 2 or more years.	Person who has two or more living grandparents.	Person who has attended a Bar or Bar Mitzvah.

Figure 2.16   Bingo (from Kaagan 1999: 146)

ethnic differences (Thiagarajan 2006: 209). The game has the follow-ing, so-called, flow: First, an incomplete sentence is written on the blackboard. It reads: I am an ... The participants are then invited to complete the sentence inside their heads as a way to distinguish themselves from others. Subsequently, they write down this word or phrase on a piece of paper. This is repeated 10 times so that, in the end, each participant has 10 phrases of self-description. All the lists are then mixed together on a table and each of the participants randomly picks one (not their own). They are given a sheet of paper with a list of categories of differences. Now, the participants have to sort through the phrases on their paper according to the categories they have been given, and they are invited to discuss the categorical affiliation of the phrases. Then follows a discussion of what characterizes the most popular and least popular categories of difference and whether there are certain phrases that do not at all fit the listed categories so that new categories have to be defined. The list of categories of differences looks like this:

Activity level (couch potato)
Age (senior citizen)
Association membership
  (Mensa member)
Astrological sign (Aries)
Belief (pro-life proponent)
Birth order (first born)
Ethnicity (Hispanic)
Family type (person from at
  large family)
Gender (woman)
Interest (mystery-story reader)
Language (Spanish speaker)
Marital status (divorced woman)
National origin (African)
National politics (Democrat)

Organization (IMB employee)
Personal characteristic
  (impatient person)
Personality type (introvert)
Physical characteristic (tall person)
Political ideology (capitalist)
Profession (trainer)
Professional approach
  (behaviourist)
Race (Caucasian)
Region (Southerner)
Religion (Roman Catholic)
Social class (underprivileged)
Socioeconomic status (yuppie)
Thinking style (analytical)
Tribe (Kpelle)

Management is another large theme for games within this strategy, and the overriding notion is that good management has to be played into existence. One example of such a game is 'Leadership advice' in which the points of departure are the participant's personal role models for management taken from work, family, sports, or elsewhere. The participants choose a role model and write down his or her name. Then they are asked to fully enter the role of this character as they define his or her characteristics and, based on this role, give advice to an imagined young manager. Subsequently, the participants swap role model cards and have to now play someone else's role model. The game develops in stages by defining the result of the previous stage as the object of play and reflection. First, role models are picked, then advice is given, then roles are swapped, then the advice is compared, etc. (Thiagarajan 2006: 173–175). Gradually, the game creates not only specific advice but also a number of perspectives from which advice can be given and a pool of different reflections upon these perspectives and the advice they engender.

There are large numbers of change games. Luke Hohman, for example, has written a book just about innovation games (Hohmann 2007). Michael Schrage defines the relation between innovation and play in this way: 'You can't be a serious innovator unless you are willing and able to play ... The essence of serious play is the challenge and thrill of confronting uncertainties' (Schrage 2000: 2). Similarly, Mark Dodgson, David Gann and Ammon Saltzer see play as central to innovation: 'The concept of play enables the link between ideas and action. Play is the medium between thinking and doing ... Play is the linchpin between the generation of new ideas and their articulation in practice ... Play gives shape to ideas, enabling selection, manipulation and learning about possibilities and focusing the mind of doers on action' (Dodgson, Gann & Saltzer 2005: 138). Some of the change games are designed to create an innovative perspective in employees, other are meant to deal with resistance to change, and still others to play strategies for change into existence. One of these games is called 'Change the picture and the paradigm'. The purpose of the game is to encourage the participants to move flexibly between different paradigms. Each participant begins by choosing a picture. Then, they are asked to cut up the picture so that it looses its original identity. Subsequently, they are asked to put the picture back together again as a form of collage. The only rule is that it cannot be re-assembled into the original picture. Each participant then has to present his or her new picture to the group and explain what the picture was before its transformation. Then the group discusses what it felt like to transform one picture into another and whether it was difficult to free oneself from the original. Finally, the group discusses on a more general level what it means to reject one paradigm and adapt to or create another. The participants are also invited provide examples of organizational or personal paradigm shifts (Scannell, Newstrom & Nilson 1998).

Scanning across the total sum of themes within the different strategies, one is struck by how many organizational themes are articulated as themes for games. If we distinguish, as we did at the beginning of this chapter, between a factual dimension (articulation of factual relations and objects), a temporal dimension (articulation of the relation past/present/future) and a social dimension (as the articulation of identity and us/them relations), then all three dimensions become reflected through play.

The *factual dimension* is reflected particularly in games about perspectives. That is to say, the games do not reflect the fact itself. They also do not reflect particular perspectives on the fact. They reflect the very notion of having perspectives and the ability to switch between perspectives. The games open up playing with perspectives. How to observe the matters of fact becomes play.

The temporal dimension is reflected particularly in games that concern projections into an undefined future. Again, they are not a specific time period. They are sometimes concerned with defining a specific future, e.g. as a vision, a challenge, or a strategy. Above all, however, the games reflect the notion of defining one in the future, that is, to create a future of the present and a future of the future. The games are concerned with the ability to create one's time. These games typically differentiate themselves in relation to the temporal dimension of different systems: the time of the team, the time of the organization, the time of the partnership, the time of the employee, and personal time. The games presume that actors live their lives heading towards an imagined future. So the reality of present is determined by the virtuality of the future, and what the games tries to do is to make the virtual visible: to open up the stage of the present by playing with the future(s).

The social dimension, however, is by far the most often represented and reflected in play. Once again, the games are often about the attainment of specific roles through the acquisition of specific preconditions. Almost all the games focus on self-creation, on the capacity for creating oneself and ones fate in the form of social relations, self-relation and personal development. Thus, these games move across the distinctions us/them and self/other, and the games are not simply concerned with the ability to define oneself but with the ability to manage these distinctions in variously embedded forms. It is a question of playing parts of oneself into life and establishing the self as a playing self that can never be fully fixed. The self has to be able to keep on playing with itself and about itself. Some of the games focus on supporting self-images. Thus, the relation between self and other becomes reintroduced into itself. One becomes a self through the act of relating to images of oneself. In that way, these self-images turn into oneself as the other for oneself. Other games establish images of the other, and the self becomes the negative of these. In yet other games, other participants create images of oneself in a way so that the self is played forth through the mirroring of others images of oneself. Similarly, with the us/them distinction in relation to teambuilding games in which the games are both about imagining the them in relation to whom one becomes an us and about them in us, that is to say, the way in which even within a team some are defined as fundamentally outside. In this way, we arrive at other various re-entries such as the self itself, the self's other, the other's other, etc. Here, organization, membership and personality are established through play. How to develop one self becomes a game, and games become a play of selves among playful selves.

What Table 2.3 indicates is that the relation between play and reality is radically displaced in relation to the semantic of the preceding phase. Indeed, reality as reality is articulated fundamentally differently to that in the preceding phase. In the preceding phase, games were supposed to be realistic, that is, represent a reality, perceived as external to the reality of the game. That led to two dilemmas between simplification/realism and playability/realism respectively. Today's semantics is not crowded by passive receptive words such as representation but instead with active words for creation and production. The games and exercises are consistently described in terms such as to build, shape, develop, grow, renew, emerge and transform. The games do not simply play with a reality. They are considered actual reality. Alanna Jones, for example, writes: 'When they play a game, they have to act that way. The game is real. It shows what the participant really does. If there is a problem, you can address the behaviours as they occur. You don't have to talk about a past that is gone or a speculative future' (Jones 1996: 2). The game is reality and creates reality in the form of personalities, social relations, in temporal perspectives and as cognitive perspectives on the world.

Games in the preceding phase implied a form of realistic epistemology of reality as it really existed. The current semantics seem to adhere to the implicit epistemology of ascribing to being a fluid character and a surplus of possibilities. It is an ontology in which being is seen as emergent, that is, something which is continually in a state of becoming. Newstrom & Scannell, for example, in their book about

Table 2.3 Examples of themes distributed according to dimensions of meaning

Social dimension	Factual dimension	Temporal dimension
Us/them	Creative thinking	Articulation of goals
Network formation	Customer satisfaction	Planning
Team work	Project selection	Vision, mission, identity
Team spirit	Paradigm shifts	Personal future and goals
Mutual responsibility	Benchmarking	Stories
Agreement	Value enhancement	Strategy
Mutual understanding	Performance criteria	
Team learning		
Mutual trust		
Raising collective courage and morale		
I/me		
Self-esteem		
Self-knowledge		
Positivity		
Empowerment		
I/us		
Personal tensions		
Emotional communication		
Sharing of emotions		
Change of roles		

teambuilding, observe teams as constantly under the threat of their own uncertainty, which manifests itself as waste, loss of energy, frustration, and boredom (Newstrom & Scannell 1998: xiii–xiv). In that context, games are seen as productive. Newstrom & Scannell believe that members expectations of a team are that it will be vigorous, characterized by intensity, innovative, engaging and imaginative. In other words, member expectations are expected to be of second-order. Members are expected to continually expect the creation of expectations. And games are considered to be able to accomplish just that.

4. Conclusion

Clearly, the effort to connect play and organization is not a recent development, but the articulated connections enter through some radical shifts.

Table 2.4 Semantic history

Time	Forms of play	The relation play/reality	The function of play
1860 onwards	Competitive games	Play symbolizes the reality of the organization	Amplification of the organization's rules
1955 onwards	Training and simulation games	Play has to strive towards a simplified representation of the organizational reality	Training and testing of competent adoption of roles
1980 onwards	Social creation games	Play *is* reality and facilitates interactional creation of the organizational reality	Invitation to play the organization and its social relations into existence

In the first phase from the 1860s onwards, it is mostly competitive games that are seen as relevant to the organization. Competitions of various kinds are organized between organizations, between employees and between customers. These competitions are organized but they are not in themselves organizing. Competitive games constitute a specific form of doubling of what was considered to be the essence of market economy and of the industry: competition. Competitive games symbolized market economy as the unavoidable reality of organizations. At the same time, however, competitive games were not competition itself. They were set free from a specific purpose. Competitions were organized for the sake of competition itself. This was their playful element. And precisely for that reason, competitive games were able to serve a more general purpose, which was to increase motivation. At the same time, these games were perceived as a way to bring into focus the object of the competition, which is why they were able to serve as a form of disciplining of competition on a more general level. Contrary to market competition, competitive games have visible and explicit rules and it is evident who is the winner and what it takes to win. Paradoxically, therefore, these games function as a way to support an effort to give an abstract notion of competition a concrete and visible form by means of its opposite, that is, play.

In the second phase, the semantic is radically different. Games are designed for purposes of training a specific group of students, employees or managers to assume specific organizational roles and functions such as decision maker or negotiator. A game is perceived in opposition to case. One learns from cases. Games, on the other hand, allows for the individual to experience on his or her own while learning. Therefore, the games are not meant to simply symbolize certain aspects of the organizational reality. The games are to represent reality in a way so that experiences can become realistic.

In the third phase, we can trace another radical shift. These games are not simply organized play but play that is meant to be organizing. The organization perceived as social relations, visions, strategies, roles and identities is to be played into existence. The games become social creation games. Reality is not represented through play. Play is reality, and the organizational reality has to be played into existence. In other words, we have a reality of play.

3
The Organization at Play

Introduction

The emergence of social creation games raises a range of questions. The question that I will focus on is: In what ways do creation games implicate organizational conditions for the creation of organizational unity and integration?

With this question, I also shift my analytical perspective. In the preceding chapter, my perspective was semantic and my focus was the conceptual formation of the relation between play and organization. This chapter is primarily form-analytical and secondarily coupling-analytical. I analyse play and decision respectively as two distinctive forms of communication each with their own communicative logic. I enquire into the way in which these two forms of communication are thought to be coupled in creation games and the implications of this for the possible unfolding of decision as form and the organizational creation of unity.

Form analysis

When there is communication, that communication always assumes a form. Communication makes distinctions, and we refer to the unity of distinctions as form. Society has a historical limited (but not given) number of basic forms of communication, e.g. morality, law, contract, and gift giving. A *communication form* can be defined as the unity of a specific differentiating operation in the communication (Luhmann 1999). A transaction, for example, indicates the unity of payment and non-payment. Every economic communication continually draws up this kind of distinction. A legal decision indicates the unity of right and wrong. A contract is the unity of mutual obligation and freedom. Other forms could be care, forgiveness, and love. The communication forms each have their own communicative logics and their own mutually exclusive way of continually splitting communication into differences between marked and unmarked. When analyzing communication forms, one should ask: Which difference does it operate within, and which form holds the difference together in a unity? This comprises of certain sub-questions. If x is indicated, what is the difference's other side? That is, what is located on either side of the difference? What kind of tension exists between the two sides? How is it possible for communication to continue to operate within the same distinction? How is the difference's blind spot defined? How does it define the conditions of impossibility for the continuation of the communication? Which observer emerges when the observer operates within the difference? And more generally, how is the *form* of communication defined which a system can create and unfold by means of and which is repeated in all of the system's operations, elements, and distinctions?

Every form establishes a paradox (Luhmann 1993d, 1999). A form separates what cannot naturally be separated. The relation between the inside and the outside of the form is always a relation of impossibility so that the objective of a form analysis is to specify the communication form's specific conditions of impossibility on the basis of which the communication is forced to create possibilities. The paradox of the communication form is also its autopoietical machinery. The form of law, for example, is right/wrong. The paradox of law is that it can never be fully decided whether the difference right/wrong is itself right or wrong. This undecidability means that every communication of right or wrong is always unstable and contains an element of undecidability. A decision about right or wrong always proves volatile and never completely holds up. That compels communication to move on in still new efforts to fix the difference. It is a question of the non-completable inner logic of the forms of communication and operations. In other words, a form analysis explores the basic differences through which communication operates and which causes all communication within the form to settle on either the inside or the outside of the form. The form establishes expectations with respect to the continuation of the communication. However, precisely because these expectations are framed within a difference, there is always a point where the expectations break down. The objective of the form analysis is to display this inner logic in a specific form of communication. It is a question of the boundary of the formation of expectations given a particular split operation in the communication.

Coupling analysis

Forms of communication are operatively closed. The law creates itself on the basis of legal operations and is unable to use economic transaction operations as a way to decide right and wrong. Law and economy cannot communicate with each other in the sense of linking up with each other's operations of distinction. They can, however, interfere with each other by observing each other. Teubner (1991) defines this by saying that a system can productively misread another system's communication. The law may for example communicate about a defendant's economic activities without fundamentally understanding the economic aspects of these activities and instead fasten upon the motives behind the crime. Another example could be that the legal system communicates a number of new rulings in which corporate discharge of waste is deemed illegal and fines are issued. This is of course observable in the economic system of communication, but only in terms of economy. The legal communication is productively (mis)understood as price determination of waste discharge. Luhmann refers to this by saying that systems are operatively closed but cognitively open (Luhmann 1992). The coupling analysis is precisely an analysis of the mutual conditions of interruption between differences in systems of communication.

Accordingly, the guiding difference in the coupling analysis is between coupling and differentiation. It studies couplings of differentiated systems. The analysis is about specifying the way in which systems allow themselves to be interrupted by each other in their operative closure in relation to one another. The systems theory is highly sensitive to systems relations because it does not consider them 'natural'. Because systems are seen as operatively closed, systems theory achieves a high level of sensitivity to the 'mechanisms' that do after all create mutual couplings. If communication between systems is not given, one develops a sharper eye for the character of systems relations. Thus, the question posed by the coupling analysis is: In which ways are systems coupled while simultaneously maintaining their differentiation?

Luhmann identifies that systems of communication are autopoietical systems, which create all the elements that they consist of (Luhmann 1995). A system is unable to produce elements for another system. A system can only produce its own internal order. It cannot produce order for others. A system of communication is operatively closed in that its operations link up recursively with previous operations in the system. On the other hand, a system is cognitively open through observation. Systems are able to observe their environment, including other systems, but they are unable to operate in the environment, including other systems. This also implies on a more general level that the systems cannot communicate with one another. They simply draw different boundaries of meaning, that is, they produce meaning in different ways. They can observe each other's communication. They can also ascribe meaning to each other's communication but only on the basis of their own forms of communication.

The fact that systems cannot communicate with each other but are able, in turn, to observe each other makes structural couplings between them possible. Structural couplings are forms of simultaneous operations. Couplings can provide systems with a continual flow of disorder up against which the systems can create and change themselves.

Couplings are always only couplings in relation to mutually closed systems. Structural couplings presuppose systems differentiation. However, this difference between coupling and differentiation has to also be a part of the very form of coupling. A coupling cannot be defined as occurring in the space that exists between systems. A coupling has to be located within the individual systems and has to there to hold together and separate the systems. A structural coupling between systems of communication can be defined simply as the unity of irritation from other systems and indifference towards other systems (Luhmann 1992: 1433). Therefore, a coupling analysis has to specify the way in which a coupling opens up towards a particular form of irritation of a system of communication within the system itself and, at the same time, the way that the coupling ensures indifference so that the system does not experience a complete collapse due to irritation. I have formalized the structural coupling's general form which is shown in Figure 3.1.

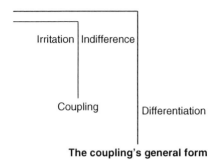

Figure 3.1   Structural coupling

There is no deterministic relation between communication form and semantic reservoir, in the sense that a communication in the form of decision can only employ concepts from an organizational semantics or that religious beliefs can only be articulated in theological concepts. It is also not reversely deterministic in the sense that only communication of religious beliefs link up with theological semantics. To the extent that a political communication perceives theological concepts as applicable, there is nothing to prevent such application, although it obviously has a significant impact on the specific content assigned to the concepts in the communication. The relation is not, on the other hand, fully arbitrary. One could say that the semantics make themselves attractive to particular forms of communication. And this is what we will explore here – the way in which the semantics of creation games makes itself attractive to play and decision as distinct forms of communication and the way that the semantics encourages different couplings between forms of communication.

First, I will analyse play as a form, then decision as form, and subsequently the way in which they interrupt each other.

1. Play as form

Let us begin by looking at play as form. Is play a particular form of communication and, if so, which form? How does play operate communicatively and through which difference? How do we define the 'eigen-logic' of play?

In sociology, most literature about play is characterized by first-order observations. There are no observations of the perception of the world through play. Play is often observed as a function of something else. This applies for example to Mead's theory about play and games, where play is thought to serve a higher purpose regarding the formulation of a theory of personality formation. Mead writes, for example: 'When the child plays, its behaviour fully expresses the role that it has activated in itself' (Mead 2005: 188, my translation). Thus, to Mead, play is a function of socialization and personality formation. Different sociological theories about play as a function of something else seems in a peculiar way to be associated with different philosophical observations about play, in particular Hans-Georg Gadamer's hermeneutic theory of play, which perceives play as an essentially independent phenomenon. Here, play seems to be defined as the exception to functionalism. Play is indeed seen as something in itself, but the notion that play can be observed as 'its own game' is seen as precisely the unique element of play. The theory generally implies, therefore, that a number of social phenomena are defined by factors external to their functionality. However, play serves precisely no other purpose than the ones defined by play while playing. According to Gadamer, play has its own spirit (Gadamer 1985: 96), or as he writes in *Truth and Method*: 'Play ... is not tied to any goal which would bring it to an end ... The movement which is play has no goal which brings it to an end; rather it renews itself in constant repetition. The movement backwards and forwards is obviously so central for the definition of a game that it is not important who and what performs this movement The movement of play as such has, as it were, no substrate' (Gadamer 1985: 93). Hence, what is special about play is that it originates in itself, which also means that play cannot be controlled by the intentions of its players. Play frees itself from subjective intentions behind the play by providing its players with the opportunity to forget themselves in play (Gadamer 1985: 92, Wind 1987: 45). Serious play means to forget oneself in play.

Both Mead and Gadamer provide first-order observations of play. In Mead's case because play is observed as a function defined outside play and in Gadamer's case because play is observed as a universal essence, which in turn can function as the foundation of the independence of other forms, particularly aesthetics and arts to the extent that these fields in their works are true to the nature of play.

I am going to take another direction. It is a question of observing the way in which observation and communication take place through play. My proposal for an observation of the form of communication of play is primarily indebted to Johan Huizinga and Gregory Bateson who both, but in two distinct ways, have carried out second-order observations of play. On the basis of their observations and in Luhmann's form terminology, I am going to propose the observation of play as a form of communication.

In 1936 [1971], Johan Huizinga published the probably most famous book about play, *Homo Ludens*, that is, playing man. Huizinga studies play as an independent cultural phenomenon, i.e. play as an independent form that cannot be reduced to other forms. The first part of the book explores the possibility of seeing play as an aspect of other forms. He looks at obvious distinctions such as play/seriousness, play/intelligence/stupidity and play/morality. He concludes in the introductory study: 'The more we try to mark off the form we call "play" from other forms apparently related to it, the more the absolute independence of the play-concept stands out' (Huizinga 1971: 6) In his analysis of the relation between play and seriousness, Huizinga defines seriousness as the negation of play but argues that the opposite does not apply: 'Play is a thing by itself. The play-concept as such is of a higher order than is seriousness. For seriousness seeks to exclude play, whereas play can very well include seriousness' (Huizinga, 1971: 45). Play, says Huizinga, is characterized as being fundamentally superfluous (Huizinga 1971: 8). By this he means precisely that the meaning of play derives from play itself. It is not a function of another form. It is not a task.

According to Huizinga, there are a number of characteristics of play as a distinctive form. One of the most important characteristics is that play is free and voluntary. One cannot play on command: 'Play to order is no longer play: it could at best be but a forcible imitation of it' (Huizinga 1971: 7). Moreover, play is always 'pretend-play': 'Play is not 'ordinary' or 'real' life. It is rather a stepping out of 'real' life into a temporary sphere of activity with a disposition all of its own. Every child knows perfectly well that he is 'only pretending', or that it was 'only for fun'' (Huizinga 1971: 8). According to Huizinga, play always plays itself out within its own space. Play has its own isolated space and its own self-defined temporality. Each act of play moves within its own play-space and begins and ends itself. Or as Huizinga writes: 'Play begins, and at a certain moment it is "over". It "plays itself out"' (Huizinga 1971: 10). This can also be termed play as self-creating order. Play creates order and is itself order (Huizinga 1971: 10). Huizinga sums up the form of play in this way: 'Summing up the formal characteristic of play we might call it a free activity standing quite consciously outside "ordinary" life as being "not serious", but at the same time absorbing the player intensely and utterly. It is an activity connected with no material interest, and no profit can be gained by it. It proceeds within its own proper boundaries of time and space according to fixed rules and in an orderly manner. It promotes the formation of social groupings which tend to surround themselves with secrecy and to stress their difference from the common world by disguise or other means' (Huizinga 1971: 13).

Whereas Huizinga observes play as cultural form, Bateson observes play as a distinctive form of communication (Bateson 2000). Thus Bateson provides a distinction (albeit implicit) between play as a specific communicative operational form on one side and the semantics of play and culture on the other side, perceived as those structures which in different contexts and at different times are available to play as form. Bateson most specifically discusses the form of play in two articles (both in: Bateson 2000). One is 'About Games and Being Serious', which is a meta-logue between Bateson and his daughter. The other one is a more comprehensive article entitled 'A Theory of Play and Fantasy', which concludes with some thoughts on the relationship between play and therapy. The analysis of play is simply drawn into a discussion of the rules that psychotherapy is subject to. There are, however, a large number of common characteristics in Huizinga's and Bateson's analyses of the form of play, particularly the notion that acts of play are not what they pretend to be. Whereas Huizinga with his cultural-theoretical perspective includes many nuances and details in relation to the forms of unfolding of play and games, Bateson is much sharper in his analysis of the form logic of play.

For Bateson, play represents a particular form of communication, containing a particular paradox that continually unfolds itself in play. And he gives a rather precise description of this paradox. Bateson begins by stating that play always involves meta-communication, which communicates the fact that 'this is play'. Thus, a form-logical characteristic of any act of play is its ongoing communication about itself as play. Play continually communicates that 'this is play' or asks 'is this play'?

In his further definition of the form of play, he seeks to explore what kind of distinction is made when stating that 'this is play'. He first suggests: 'Expanded, the statement "This is play" looks something like this: These actions in which we now engage do not denote what those actions *for which they stand* would denote' (Bateson 2000: 180). When children play-fight, they continually draw up a distinction between play-fighting and fighting, and that distinction is made by the notion that the marked strike signifies the strike but does not signify that which a strike would signify. Bateson's final and more formally precise formulation is: 'These actions in which we now engage, do not denote what would be denoted by those actions which these actions denote' (Bateson 2000: 180).

This way of defining play, however, contains an inherent paradox or condition of impossibility. This paradox has to do with the difficulty in play of delimiting itself: 'This is play' sets a frame for the act of play, an inside and an outside of play, which says 'pay attention to what is inside and do not pay attention to what is outside' (Bateson 2000: 184–185). The inherent paradox consists in the fact that the frame cannot escape its part in the act of play since the frame is precisely defined in the game by virtue of the question 'Is this play?' Play makes up its own rules, but as soon as play begins to play with its rules, it also plays with its frame and it becomes clear where the play ends. To return to the example of play-fighting, one could say that the strike, which is not a strike, is not always easily recognizable. Play-fighting has the potential to quickly turn into actual fighting, where strikes denote what they usually denote. Play-fighting continually explores what marks the marked strike and this establishes the game and its rules. Play plays, but it also continually puts its own constitution to the test. Only in play can it be determined whether play is play, which means whether to continue or discontinue the game.

Articulated in our form-analytical discourse, we might propose that play is a form of communication as the unity of the difference between 'These actions in which we now engage do not denote what those actions for which they stand would denote' and 'These actions in which we now engage, denote what these actions denote'. Play always defines its outside as 'These actions in which we now engage, denote what these actions denote'. The outside represents that with which one can play but which play cannot be. Play has to always continue on the inside of the difference in order to continue to be play. However, the problem for play is that this difference is not given and is often difficult to establish. Therefore, we see a so-called re-entry of the difference where the difference becomes a part of its own unity. In order to have play, one has to play, so to speak, with the difference between play and non-play, which means that the incompleteness of the form of play both ensures and threatens the continuation of play. It can be formalized as shown in Figure 3.2.

Thus, play represents a distinct communicative doubling machine. Play doubles the world so that we have a world of play and a real world, and the doubling takes place on the side of play. That is, the real is not the real as such but the real world as its look like from the perspectives of play. The real world observed through the form of play is the reality that the form of play plays with. Dirk Baecker formulates it in this way: 'In play, socialness is constituted by ways of reflection onto itself as the other side of itself. In play, socialness is experienced as what it is, namely as contingent, roughly meaning that it is neither necessary nor impossible, or again, given yet changeable. Play in general reveals the form of the social by which the play infects the world (Baecker 1999: 103). Play represents a communicative socialness characterized by its doubling of this socialness so that the contingency of the social reality becomes visible.

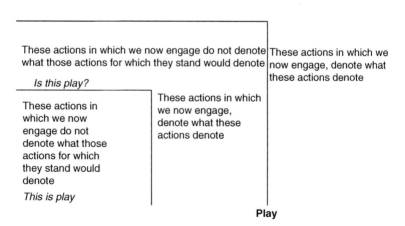

Figure 3.2 The form of play

This obviously makes specific demands on potential communication participants. Someone is only relevant to the communication to the extent that they are willing to play along, and to play along also means to double oneself as player and as one's personality outside the game. As a player, one has to be prepared not only to observe the contingency of the world but to see oneself as contingent. The 'playing self' puts 'the real self' in parenthesis and that makes it possible to freely act out different roles in play without being held responsible at the end of the game. I only pretended to be Darth Vader. However, pretending to be Darth Vader also necessarily suggest the possibility of pretending to be oneself; that is, to see the contingency of the manifestation of the self.

Fantasy might be observed as the communication media of play. Play always has to put something at stake by elevating the obvious to something contingent. Play lives by the tensions putting something at stake. It brings energy to the play. And fantasy is in play constructed as the spring of imagining contingency. In this sense 'the serious' is not something opposed to play. Play has to be serious in dealing with tensions. Alternatively play dies in boredom losing its energy.

2. Decision as form

Decision is a very different form of communication, which in each of its operations divides the world in a particular way. Referring to Luhman's analysis of the form of decision, I suggest an observation of decision as communication that implies an *assessment* of social expectations (Luhmann 1993a). There is a multitude of different expectations continually circulating within each communication, including temporal expectations, factual expectations, and social expectations. Social expectations are directed towards communication participants, expectations concerning 'them', 'me', and 'us', etc. Decisions can be directed at anything but they only impact on the social organization of expectations. Decisions are directed towards expectations in the communication but do not function as a representation of the expectations in themselves. Decision communication is precisely the *assessment* of the many different and perhaps even conflicting expectations in the organization communication.

Decisions do no determine the future. Decisions stipulate and direct in the moment expectations among the members of the organization with respect to future directions in the organization and each member's individual role and responsibilities and in particular what can be expected of future decisions. Thus, decisions regulate social expectations concerning subsequent decisions.

Such regulation of expectations is achieved when a decision operation draws a distinction within the communication between a before and an after the decision. A decision splits the world into a 'before' and an 'after'. The distinction between before and after is a distinction within the deciding decision operation. When the decision decides, it indicates that we are 'now' 'after' the decision. Not until the decision has been made is it possible to cross the boundary between before and after and refer to 'before' as being located before the decision. Therefore, 'before' always exists in the order of observation of the 'after'. It has to be that way. 'Before' is always relative to the decision's indication that something has been decided. Therefore, 'before' is constantly moving in relation to the indication of new decisions within the communication.

From the perspective of the decision, 'before the decision' is defined as a space of *open contingency* with respect to which social expectations among the organizational members will assert themselves in the future. The 'before' of the decision is defined as a space where one can imagine many different solutions to a specific situation, where much can still be changed. After the decision is made, this contingency and openness concerning solutions to the situation appear in fixed form, as the notion that the decision could have been made differently. Only one solution was actually decided on, but other solutions could have been chosen. What could have been changed has now been determined. We could have done many different things, but we chose to do this one thing. In this way, decision communication shapes in every one of its operations the difference fixed/open contingency with respect to social expectations (Luhmann 1993a). The formalized form of decision is shown in Figure 3.3.

In effect, a decision represents the unity of the difference fixed/open contingency with respect to social expectations, and as unity a decision is both what divides the world into two sides and that which holds it together. This means that every decision not only regulates expectations, it also produces uncertainty because it becomes clear that the decision could have been made differently. Social contingency is both fixed and opened up through the operation

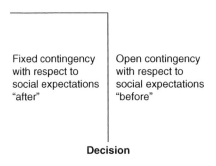

Decision

Figure 3.3   The form of decision

of the decision since the fixed and regulated expectations always appear on a horizon of other potential regulations. Therefore, new potential decisions come into being at the moment a decision is made, which implies the appearance of new possible links for further communication.

There are certain inherent paradoxes in the form of decision communication. One paradox is the fact that decisions regulate social expectations concerning the future, but that they are always made retrospectively. Not until a decision has been carried out is it possible to determine whether it was actually made, whether expectations were regulated, or whether the contingency was fixed or not. The point is that the decision does not assume facticity as a decision until a possible subsequent decision is apparent. Only in retrospect is it possible to determine if a decision was in fact a decision or just talk, regardless of what the communication 'originally' referred to. This also means that decisions constantly make decisions about which previous communications were in fact decisions and therefore can be granted the status of decision premises for future decisions. In other words, not until a decision is recognized as a decision premise has it been decided. Decision communication is not only communication *within* the form of decision, therefore, but always already communication *about* decisions (Luhmann 2000: 222–256).

Moreover, decision communication is paradoxical in the sense that only fundamentally undecidable questions can be objects of decisions (Foerster 1989, 1992, Luhmann 1993a, Luhmann 2000: 132). It is not possible to calculate one's way to the only right decision. Decisions always potentialize alternative decisions and always contain, therefore, something undecided. Only if it were possible to completely deduct, calculate, or argue one's way to a decision would the decision lead to final closure or fixing of contingency without potentializing alternatives. However, if such factual analysis leads to a result it would precisely not be a decision but instead merely calculation and deduction. Decisions exist in a space of freedom that cannot be analysed away.

Finally, decision communication can be said to be paradoxical to the extent that the question of what defines a decision in itself has to be given in the form of a decision. In organizations, only the decision can decide when something is a decision, that is, when something is a fixing of social expectations. Therefore, organizations do not simply make decisions. They also continually make decisions about what makes a decision a decision. Who, for example, is authorized to make which decisions? The question of when a social expectation becomes fixed is not given. Decisions have to decide themselves and always leave a remnant of undecidability.

The inherent paradox in the form of decision is also the autopoietical machinery of organizational systems. Because a decision cannot be made singularly, once and for all, but instead continually potentializes alternatives and creates doubt about its character of decision, decisions have to constantly be followed up by new decisions. Because decisions cannot be made, their paradox has to be continually dissolved into cascades of new decisions. This is the driving force of organizational systems. They are forced to continually create decision communication. When decisions link up with previous decisions, they are transformed into decision premises for further decisions, and this is what makes an organization. Organizations are nothing but a concomitant byproduct of the unfolding of the paradoxy of the form of decision. Organizations and their elements such as employment, structures, objective, strategies, visions, etc. are created through decision communication as decisions confirm decisions and turn them into decision premises for new decisions. *What* an organization is and consist of follows from *how* the organization deparadoxifies decisions and converts them into decision premises.

In my discussion of play I spoke about the way in which the subject is defined through play. In the form of play, the subject is played forth while playing. In play, one is not a predefined subject. Play turns the player into a subject by offering the player the possibility of doubling herself. It is different in decision communication. In decision communication the subject is presupposed as preceding the decision. A decision refers to a subject outside the decision to whom the decision can be assigned and who can be observed as decision maker. The subject functions within the decision communication as decision premise.

3. Can decisions be playful?

There is a lot of communication in any organization that is not observed as decisions and hence organized and converted into premises for further decisions. Luhmann speaks of interaction systems as systems of communication, which are constituted by simultaneity and dissolve when this simultaneity seizes to apply. Three employees meet by the coffee maker and chat about their plans for the summer. This communication takes place in the context of an organization. The organization has made it possible for them to meet by the coffee maker. However, their communication is not necessarily a part of the organization. Their chat is only relevant to the extent that new communications link up with it as a decision premise. Perhaps the discussion of summer plans is perceived in a new retrospective communication as premise for a coordinating decision about who is going to take their vacation when, which means that the coffee break turned out not to be a coffee break after all. A meeting, in fact, is also an interaction system. Obviously, a meeting is also an element in the organizational system to the extent that it has been decided and been assigned a valid agenda. At the same time, however, when employees meet, an interaction system is established. A meeting can include many different topics. Only the part of the meeting that is subsequently assigned the status of decision becomes part of the organization. That is why meetings often begin with the approval of minutes. This is a way to define the decision from the last meeting as actual decisions, which then function as the premises for the current meeting.

There is ample communication in organizations, but the organization is only created through the selection of communication in the flow of decisions, that is, what is decided as decisions and what is not. However, this does not put an end to the difficulties the organization encounters in its effort to create itself and its unity since every decision tends to open up a cascade of new decisions, in the same way that meetings tend to produce new meeting forums with their own agendas and meeting schedules. This is basically because every communication within the form of a decision does not simply create one possible follow-up to a decision but instead a horizon of potential links to new decisions. Decisions often become differentiated into sub-decisions that quickly forget their status of 'sub', and this produces a kind of centrifugal force within organizations. In this way, every organization is threatened by its own internal differentiation into a vast number of decision flows, which form their own systems with meetings, issues and members, and it becomes problematic not only to determine which communications represent decisions but also the status and association of these decisions. I refer to this as the problem of organizational unity.

The question of differentiation versus unity is a classic sociological question, which has been answered in many different ways. A prevailing assumption is that what holds together a system is some form of commonality: a contract; a common culture; a common lifeworld, etc. In this terminology, a system is poorly integrated if the commonality is thin, but strongly integrated if the system has the character of community. Luhmann's perspective is completely different. A system is integrated when it allows for a high degree of internal differentiation into sub-systems. When we enquire into the unity of an organization and integration, therefore, we enquire into the way in which an organization conditions freedom for differentiated decision communication and hence to the way in which the organization reduced the overproduction of sub-systemic possibilities (Luhmann 1996: 344–345). The greater the level of difference an organization is able to tolerate, the more integrated it is.

This condition pertains of course fundamentally to decisions that ascribe decisions to the organization. In the traditional bureaucratic organization this happens through decided self-descriptions of the organization as a specific hierarchy. When the organization describes itself as hierarchy, it decides the premises for the force of decision in differentiated and subordinated decisions. In other words, it conditions the level of freedom for organizational sub-systems.

Today, hierarchical forms of integration have come under pressure because organizations are increasingly expected to be able to adapt to unknown conditions. They have to be prepared to be something that they are not. Today's organizations often describe their environment as increasingly complex and turbulent, and they are unable, therefore, to position themselves as hierarchical without running the risk of being incompatible with expectations in the environment. In the attempt to counter an undefined environment, the organizational structure becomes fluid and flexible, and that challenges integration. Values management, culture management and branding represent only some of the topical cognitive responses to the question of new unity; that is, unity through cognitive communities. Mintzberg's ad-hocracy figures among topical structural responses to the question of unity (Mintzberg 1993). Both kinds of response presuppose an 'outside'. In value management for example the values are decided by the organization, but in the decision they are given the status as something larger and more fundamental than the organization it self. The value becomes constructed as the constitutive outside of the organization. The first type entails designing the organizational brand or defining organizational core values, and the second type implies defining structural boundaries for delimited projects.

The question is whether play can be seen as a symptom of the problem in modern organizations with the problem of unity, and moreover, whether new forms of organizational games indicate an alternative strategy for the conditioning of freedom of differentiation? Perhaps play is an answer to the question of unity in the social dimension, which is neither cognitive nor structural and which, alone, does not presuppose a defining 'outside'? So maybe play handles the paradox of unity radically different making possible a dislocation in the very form of conditioning of freedom for subsystems?

At first, this seems unlikely to the extent that play seems incompatible with decision as form. Decisions concern the containment of uncertainty and the effort to fix social expectations. We intuitively perceive play as almost the opposite. Play places its own framework in parenthesis and doubles the world into a real world and a play-world. That does not at first seem to contribute to the fixing of social expectations.

But let us begin by observing ways in which play may become visible to decisions and then go on to define it more specifically in relation to social creation games.

The first question that presents itself is whether decisions can decide to play. All decisions can do is to assess and thus regulate social expectations. In that sense, a decision is indeed able to state 'we are going to play *Moovers*'. When children get together, they might have very different ideas of what they will be doing together, and they may decide first to play *Warhammer* and then go to jump on the trampoline. However, decisions themselves cannot play. Only play can play, and this defines a clear meaning boundary for the decision. The decision can state 'We are going to play *Warhammer*', but it cannot play *Warhammer* and therefore cannot determine whether its decision results in play, even if the children bring out their Warhammer figures, or whatever the nature of the game might be.

An organization can decide that its members are going to play 'Diversity bingo', 'Trust me', or 'So much in common', but it cannot decide whether its decision results in play. The decision may also establish rules and framework for play. But again, the communication of play has its own life and defines its own framework and rules. Only the game can frame itself. The game may of course decide to appropriate the decided framework and transform it into its own play elements, but a decision is unable to control that. A decision-based insistence upon specific frameworks and rules merely runs the risk that the game never turns into a game. One might ask, however, what the point is of deciding to play if the objective still is to decide. There are, therefore, many issues that may prevent the creation games from ever becoming play.

The creation games imply, as we have seen, that organizational elements are created through play. Strategies, visions, personal identities, team identity, roles, priorities, attitudes, and perspectives are to be played into existence. The factual, temporal, and social dimensions of the organization all have to be established through play. 'Role', 'strategy' and 'vision' represent classic organizational issues. They each have a long organizational-semantic history. But what meaning do these issues take on when they are subjected to play? Are they able to maintain their semantic identity? It is important to remember that play cannot play without doubling the world into a play-world and a real world. The real world is not the real world as such, but the real world as seen from the perspective of play. Play says: 'the real world is out there, where actions mean what they denote'. Play also says: 'this is the world of play, and you should focus on that'. What does this perspective do to strategy, roles and vision? When playing with strategy, the organizational ties no longer apply. To the extent that the creation games actually result in play with organizational strategies, for example, the game does not even take place within the organization since the game establishes its own universe. The result is that it is simply no longer relevant to play's play with strategy that exists in the form of previous decisions, previous strategies, and parallel activities in other department, etc. It is also no longer relevant what it takes for a strategy to become a strategy since that can be played with as well. What might an organization possibly gain from this? Through play, the organization is able to free itself from itself! The autopoiesis of play represents the organization's possibility of circumventing itself as a restriction and barrier for its own adaptability.

The doubling logic of play applies also to employees playing. One cannot be oneself in the game. One becomes doubled when engaging in play and is given the possibility to play someone else while remaining the same. One is given the chance to play with one's self. And again: the organization can engage its employees regardless of who they are. Play disregards employees as real entities with habits, identity and history so that these elements do not come to impede self-change. The employees simply have to participate in the game and play with their selves.

If the point is that this allows the organization to free itself from itself as constricting ties for the production of itself, this seems to be associated with some rather radical implications. The first implication seems to be that the creation games displace the organizational production of premises in the direction of differentiated play interaction, which transforms the organization into a vulnerable entity. The organization does not play; rather, it is the many games that play elements into existence, which are then assigned to the organization. The second implication concerns the organization's self-stabilizing efforts and contains the question whether play can be considered binding. It is doubtful whether the organization is able to stabilize itself by reifying the products of play through decisions. The organization may choose to dissolve the products of play in the form of new strategies, visions, etc., by making decisions about them and thus transforming them into decision premises. However, as we have seen, play has its own logic, and there is no guarantee that what represents the sustainability of its products would survive the shift to decisions. Dedication and situational engagement are among the attractive elements of play but not of decision. Or we may put it this way: The energy of play makes it binding whereas decisions, in turn, bind energy. In play, participants seem to explore the space of the highest level of energy both for the communication and the connected psychic systems. Decisions, on the other hand, seek to fix expectations. When decisions fix expectations that have been played into existence, they do not simultaneously fix the energy and dedication that was associated with those expectations in play. Therefore, a certain amount of energy is left outside the decision operation. If the organization seeks not only to fix expectations but also to stabilize and maintain the energy and dedication, the question is whether that is only possible through continued play. Accordingly: decisions are able to stabilize decisions through further decisions, and play is able to stabilize its energy through further play.

This means that the creation games can entail three entirely different implications for organizations:

Organizational play as an opening pause

First of all, creation games can establish an opening within the organization by playing possibilities into existence, which are then concluded and closed again by means of a decision that seeks to fix specific expectations, bind them in the organization, and define them as premises for new decisions. In this case, play becomes a brief outburst, a break from the organization in the way that the icebreaker strategy in particular suggests. This is the less radical introduction of play in organizations. Play is here strongly controlled by the form of decision which has the power to stop the play.

Organization at play

The second possibility is the organization's self-doubling into an organization that is played into existence and an organization that has been decided, where play represents not a brief parenthesis at a staff seminar, which quickly disappears into the past but an ongoing activity entailing decisions that continually encourage more play. And perhaps even more radically: the organization at play has on one hand a decided organization and on the other hand a multiplicity of games with their own imaginary universes. So the organization is doubled into two systems, a playing one which produces contingency and new virtual possibilities, and another one which fixes contingencies in decisions making. And the two systems in the system construct an ultra cycle of mutual productive disturbances constituting at stage of transformation.

Generalization of play

The third possibility is the most radical one. It is an organization which has *generalized* the perspective of play! Just as when Foucault talks about 'the generalization of prison' making discipline the dispositive of organizing, we might talk about a generalization of play, when play is not simply framed by decisions, but becomes a general gaze which can enlighten all aspects of the organization in any moment (Foucault 1977). It is an organization who's answer to the choice between play and decision is neither/nor and both/and because it oscillates between the two described forms; that is, between play as a break and the organization at play. This organization takes advantage of the fact that we never know whether play represents a break or the beginning of a continual process, but it is also an organization which has *generalized* the perspective of play, which means that it is possible not only to observe and reify play as decisions but also for decisions to be subsequently observed as mere play; that is, an organization, which is able to recognize differentiated communication as play even though it has never been organized and referred to as such ('no decisions were made at our meeting, but it was a fruitful process in which we brought many possibilities into play'). In this organization it is always an option to observe and communicate in the form of play with large effects of the status of the observed. In the moment of play fixed decision premises at what ever level are turned into contingencies mediated by fantasy.

4. Conclusion: deconstructive integration

Can we draw a conclusion from these observations? If so, it contains a few 'ifs'. If an organization widely employs creation games for purposes other than simply temporary suspension, and if the organization of these actually results in games that produce play, we may see the outline of a new form of integration, which we refer to as the organization at play, or *communitas ludens* to play with Huizinga's *Homo Ludens*. If such a form exists, it is a form of integration, which allows for the formation of a multiplicity of fluctuating sub-systems, playing forth prospective elements for the organization's self-creation. These prospects can either be maintained as prospects through further play or be received and organized as decided decision premises. Thus, it is a form of integration that seems to create a doubling of the organization into an official organization and a virtual multiplicity.

This form of integration can be characterized as self-deconstructive. Deconstruction does not mean destruction. The organization does not destroy itself. Rather, it is a form of integration that becomes invisible at the moment it comes into existence. It is an organization that makes it impossible for the organization to fix itself. It is a form of organization that signs away its own unambiguous unity and obtains a different multiple unity, which becomes possible precisely because it is just something we are playing; that is, because the sub-systems are the games and their results virtual. They play as an organization and simulate organization but do not constitute one. This increases the overall number of states that the organization is able to exist in and the differences it can tolerate. There is a constant production of a surplus of possibilities oscillating between the virtual and official, the non-binding and binding. The organization's capacity for being something other than what it is, perhaps even to be something other than an organization explodes.

4
Political Play with Boundaries

Introduction

Creation games imply that organizational elements are created through play. What happens if play does not only apply to individual elements in organizations but also their constitutive boundaries? That is the question addressed in this chapter. The place where play with boundaries can be seen in the most radical form and with the greatest implications is the political system. Over the past 10 years, a wealth of games has emerged within the political systems based precisely on the effort to put boundaries into play, to gamble boundaries. These boundaries do not just include boundaries between organizations and environments but also boundaries that are considered constitutive for the constitutional state. This creates a shift in our point of observation. Whereas Chapter 2 explored the semantic history of management games and focused in particular on play and games in the private sector, this chapter focuses on games that have politically regulatory objectives. I do not change my point of observation in order to establish a new subject. The subject remains creation games. The only reason for changing the point of observation is because play with boundaries can be seen to take place most radically in the political system. In this chapter I explore the way in which political organizations and public administrations make use of creation games. My thesis is that creation games are employed in the regulation of constitutive political boundaries. Creation games play with the boundaries of the political. This chapter provides examples of play within the following boundaries: voluntary organization/voluntary member; school/family; individual/community; and education/ health.

Creation games have to be seen in the context of the development of the public administration. Roughly speaking, the last 100 years of the public administration can be divided into three periods: The classic formal administration, which was formed around the end of the 1800s; the sector administration, established in the late 1950s; and the polycentric administration which slowly emerged at the beginning of the 1980s (as shown in Table 4.1) (Andersen 1995, Sand 1996, Andersen & Born 2000, 2007b, 2008, Andersen & Thygesen 2004, see also Dreier 1991, Dean 2007, Newman 2001, Clarke & Newman 1997).

The formal administration operated by means of administrative decisions and was made up, ideally, of formally delimited hierarchies in which the individual administration was delimited as a field of responsibility with the authority to make certain administrative decisions. The biggest regulatory challenge for this form of administration was to minimize the difference between rules and the practice of government officials. The form of regulation employed was the control of administrative decisions, and the regulatory object was the individual office and official. The precondition for regulation and control was the self-discipline of the individual official. The boundary of the capacity of power is drawn by the individual official's ability to single-handedly act in a systematic, experienced, and disciplined manner.

The sector administration, which emerged in the 1960s, operated through planning. Planning in this context can be defined as a second-order decision; it means to make decisions about premises for future administrative decisions. The sector administration divides and gathers different formally delimited administrative institutions into thematic sectors such as the sector for labour market policy, the sector for environmental policy and the sector for social policy. A sector is not primarily defined as a formal field of business but as a field of problems and solution horizons. Thus, sectors cut across formal boundaries and often integrate institutions of private law both in the policy formation and in the solutions. That happens, for example, in the form of corporately constituted committees, boards and councils. The sector administration formulates a regulatory problem concerning the coordination of a wealth of public sub-activities with a comprehensive sectoral perspective. The regulatory form was planning and the

Table 4.1 From formal bureaucracy to polycentry

	Operation	Delimitation	Regulatory form	Regulatory object	Regulatory boundary
Formal administration	Decision	Jurisdictive boundary	Rules/control	The practice of government officials	The self-discipline of government officials
Sector administration	Planning	Sectorial boundary	Planning	The individual administration	The administration's ability to translate centralized input into decentralized output
Polycentric administration	Strategy	Imagined boundary	Supervision	Organizational autonomy	Organizational independence and strategic capability

boundaries for planning was the expectation that the different sub-administrations responded uniformly and in a predictable way to the input from the planning so that the output from the sub-administrations came out as expected. However, the planning model collapsed in the late 1970s. It turned out that this much planning merely resulted in more planning, which increased the complexity and vagueness of the administration.

The polycentric administration gained momentum from the beginning of the 1980s and was sustained by the ideal of a public sector with adaptability on all levels. The ideal is not about adapting to any particular condition but adapting to adaptation. Clarke and Newman talk about a tyranny of transformation, where the only continuity is change itself (Clarke & Newman 1997: 39, 45). Coordination and development must be created from below by individual institutions, which are to take responsibility for their own development and for the unity they form a part of. In effect, the major regulatory problem consists in creating, from the top, adaptation from below. Today, management pertains to the adaptability of the individual institution; the ability of the individual institution to relate to itself and its own adaptation through management (Andersen 1995, Andersen & Born 2000, Rennison 2007a, 2007b, Knudsen 2005, 2006). Therefore, management obtains the character of supervision. Management becomes a question of supporting and guiding self-management. The boundary for this kind of management is the institution's capacity for independent management and strategy formation. The result is a polycentric administration without clearly defined hierarchical centres – an administration without a clear top and bottom.

The development from formal to sectoral to polycentric administration should not be seen as succeeding forms but instead as forms that build upon each other. Whereas the formal administration operates through decisions, the sector administration operates through planning in the form of decisions about premises for future decisions. In relation to this, the polycentric administration operates through strategy formation, which can be defined as decisions about premises for future planning. Strategy consists of decisions about factual perspectives and temporal horizons that define the space in which problems and solutions can be localized. The polycentric administration defines the individual administrative institution as an independent managed and strategic unit, but at the same time, there are continual negotiations about the gathering of independent institutions into imagined horizontal communities in which the independent institutions are able to bring their strategies together. These communities may be centred around integration and globalization, or around ecological sustainability, services for citizens, or something entirely different. The fundamental issue is that these communities most often function without a clear formal structure and attain their imaginary authority and cohesion by offering the institutions possibilities for development and action. These imagined communities are rather volatile. They dissolve and reconfigure themselves in competition with each other in ongoing discursive battles and campaigns. The communities cut across formal and sectoral boundaries and may include public, private and voluntary organizations, in the same way that an institution may recognize itself at different times as member of different communities. A state school, for example, may oscillate between perceiving itself as a member of a knowledge society and of a multicultural society, and depending on the community it mirrors itself in, it will see a certain set of problems, challenges, and possibilities in the same way that it will see very different potential partners in its environment. Thus, we speak today of both the network society and the network state. When today's municipalities choose to describe themselves as a network, it is precisely because the concept provides possibilities for including, in a flexible way, both private and voluntary organizations that otherwise fall outside the municipal jurisdiction. Partnerships and new forms of contracts, therefore, become points of connection in the polycentric administration (Andersen 2008a, Newman 2001, Jessop 1999).

The shift from formal administration via sector administration to polycentric administration also entails a shift in the way in which the reality of the administration is established in a meaningful way. There is a shift in the way in which time, sociality and factuality are created. Generally, in the formal administration we can speak of a *formal reality* where time is established by the tension between a factually relevant past and an externalized future. The administrative decision relates backwards. The future represents an externalized effect of the decision. In the formal administration, the social relation remains external to decision communications, and factuality is established and ordered by means of facts. Here, facts are always facts in a case about something, which means that facts are in themselves a question of decision.

By contrast, in the sector administration we can speak of a *substantial reality*. In the sector administration, time is linked to problem-solving, and problems are derived from planning-based projections from the past. In the sector administration, the social dimension is divided into problem areas, which follow the sectoral boundaries. And the factual dimension is similarly connected to the figure of the problem. Knowledge is always knowledge about a problem or a set of problems, which means that we end up with a factuality of environmental policy, a factuality of labour market policy, a factuality of taxation policy, etc. (See Table 4.2).

Table 4.2 Administrative forms of reality

	Formal administration	Sector administration	Polycentric administration
Temporal dimension	The present is stretched out between factually relevant past and externalized future	Time is linked to problem solving where present problems are derived and extrapolated from the past	The present is chosen and is stretched out between a one-dimensional past and multi-dimensional images of the future. Time becomes strategic
Social dimension	The social relation is external to social interaction	The social relation is divided into problem areas and one does not choose one's area	The social relations can and have to be chosen and re-chosen in order to leave alternatives open. The social becomes strategic
Factual dimension	Cases represent the dominant object, and facts are socially created	The policy problem is the dominant problem and all knowledge is knowledge about a problem or a set of problems.	Objects are semantic artefacts. Problems are always problems-in-perspectives. The way in which one chooses to combine artefacts becomes a strategic choice.

Finally, meaning formation in the polycentric administration is defined as strategic. We see a *strategic reality*, that is, a reality that always includes a strategic choice in the perspective on the world, which means that the world becomes defined as contingent. It can always be observed differently, which leads to other possibilities for action. Here, the present becomes stretched out between a one-dimensional, often negatively viewed, past and positive multi-dimensional images of the future. Time represents strategic formation of expectations and the social dimension is similarly defined strategically. Communities are established, chosen, and opted out of and with them different distinctions between us and them; between we who assume responsibility and the others who do not. Articulating communities such as the knowledge society, globalization, the experience economy, or the sustainable society represents ways to classify and identify players as responsible for particular perspectives and considerations. Finally, even the factual dimension becomes strategic in the polycentric administration. There is an awareness that problems are always problems-in-a-perspective, which means that perspectives are conceived as strategic artefacts.

In the formal administration, the administration observes itself by means of the difference procedure/decision, and the administration changes through change in procedures. In the sector administration, the administration observes itself by means of the difference structure/problem solving process where structure is defined as that which the administration is able to bracket and make changes to. In addition, today's administration can observe itself by means of the difference boundary/self(-adaptability), and boundaries represent that which the administration may seek to bracket and define as the object of change. The ideal about adaptability changes the very calculus of change. The sector administration makes changes on the basis of stability. It would change certain aspect of its structure while the rest remained stable. Change was observable on the basis of stability. With the ideal about adapting to adaptability, change is inserted in the place of stability. Continual change is the only stability. Adaptability, therefore, is not a question of changing certain aspects of an administration but of questioning the administrations very character of administration. It is not possible to change aspects of a boundary, and to redefine a boundary means to displace the self's conditions of emergence. Today, change is directed towards the constitutive aspect of our institutions. Projects about change in the public school do not merely concern changing certain structures and conditions but developing the very notion of what a school is and should be. From the 1980s onwards, projects about change place emphasis on the boundaries of the administration. The boundary public/private is put at stake, for example, in projects about outsourcing and public-private partnerships. The boundary of politics/administration is put at stake, for example, in group management and internal contract management. The boundary administration-employee is put at stake in the notion of the responsible employee and new practices such as performance reviews, new wages and competence agreements. The boundary public/voluntary is put at stake with new partnerships with voluntary organizations concerning public welfare responsibilities. The boundary administration/citizen is put at stake with the notion of active citizenship and self-development contracts with the individual citizen (Andersen 2007a, 2008b). The list could go on.

Where does play fit into all this? My thesis is that play may put the boundaries of the administration at stake in a new way, not only through general and central organizational decisions but through strategic orchestration of interaction. Creation games can place the strategic establishment of boundaries on the level of interaction, for example between family and school or between the organization and its employees. The politician might wish to redefine different boundaries that cannot be defined from outside. The boundary between family and school, as it is, is not only a formal boundary within the school, which the administration or the school can make decisions concerning. The school can make decisions concerning the way in which it will carry its own responsibilities, but it cannot decide how the families plan to carry out their responsibility. The school can articulate its preference for certain types of cooperation with its students' families. It can even decide that it will seek to work towards a specific format for cooperation with parents. But the school cannot decide on a specific form of cooperation. Therefore, the families' boundaries in relation to the school are established from within, in the families. Organizing play is a way for schools to invite families to redefine their boundaries in relation to the school in a way that the school considers meaningful and suitable. It is possible, for example, to publicly decide to outsource but not possible to decide the way in which companies redefine their attitude towards politics. Collective agreements can be changed, but only the employees can decide about the way in which they establish internal boundaries in relation to the organization and the way in which they feel or do not feel passionate and engaged in their work.

I wish to show by means of a number of cases the way in which political games are organized so that they are able to put constitutive boundaries at stake; boundaries which the political finds it difficult to move through authoritative decisions. I suggest that creation games represent a functional equivalent to an administration that strategizes time, sociality and factuality and puts boundaries at stake in the pursuit of increased change. It is in the nature of play to put boundaries at stake. Play always plays with boundaries and signs. The political creation games produce a generalization of the strategic reality.

1. The voluntary organization/voluntary member boundary

The first case focuses on the boundary voluntary organization/ voluntary member. The efforts over the past 20 years to integrate the voluntary organizations into the welfare state pose a challenge to the relation between voluntary organizations and their voluntary members. Increasingly, the voluntary organizations enter into contracts with public authorities in which they commit to specific activities. Below, I am going to show how voluntary organizations employ creation games in order to overcome the embarrassment that often arises when the voluntary organization enter into agreements with municipalities without the power to commit the voluntary members to these contracts. The games become a tool for engagement control of voluntary members. The organization of games is used to coordinate the voluntary members' way of defining their relationship with the voluntary organization and to personalize the boundary between the voluntary organization and its voluntary members, its users and the local community. With these games, the voluntary organizations seek to ensure that the individual volunteer defines the same boundaries in relation to the voluntary work as the organization itself, at least to the extent that the volunteer is prepared for the questions of boundaries that voluntary work entails.

Since the mid-1980s, the voluntary organizations have been granted a growing role in the development of the welfare state in

Denmark as in many other western welfare states. In particular, they have been assigned an important role in the transformation of the welfare state into a welfare society. As part of this development and initiated by the state, the Centre for Voluntary Social Work was established. The centre describes itself as a nationwide centre working to support and promote voluntary work in Denmark: 'We work from the ideal of a diverse and independent voluntary sector contributing to the welfare society in collaboration with the public sector' (Centre for Voluntary Social Work 2004: 15). Moreover, many of today's voluntary organizations enter into contracts and partnerships with public authorities, particularly municipalities, in the provision of welfare services. However, voluntary organizations often face the problem that it is difficult to enter into binding agreements about delivering specific welfare services because their workforce is voluntary. In this context, Anders la Cour speaks of the voluntary organizations as embarrassed because what they have to offer their external partners falls outside their control (la Cour 2003, Højlund & la Cour 2008). La Cour's favourite example is home visiting services. A voluntary organization may have all kinds of rules and goals for its home visiting services, but once it has sent a volunteer to someone's home its power ends because the relationship between the volunteer and the elderly quickly develops a life of its own and thus frees itself from the voluntary organization. Regardless of what the organization has agreed with the municipality about concerning practices that the volunteers are not allowed undertake, cleaning for example, the voluntary organization is helpless in a specific situation. Therefore, voluntary organizations develop alternative forms of regulation. They require a certain level of training, for example, before their volunteers are allowed to work in the field. Or they equip the volunteer with certain emblems so they can always be recognized and recognize themselves as a volunteer from a specific organization. Or, as we will see, they organize games through which they try to internalize attitudes and values in the volunteers.

We will take a closer look at two games: 'Attitudes towards volunteer policies' and 'Values at stake'. Both games are produced by the Centre for Voluntary Social Work, and the intent behind the games is that leaders of voluntary organizations can use them with their voluntary workers. Both games are about the relationship between the individual volunteer, voluntary work and the voluntary organization.

Attitudes towards volunteer policies

The game 'Attitudes towards volunteer policies' is from 2005. The game is meant to be played in the voluntary organization by its volunteers. The game consists of 66 cards and an hour timer. The game is played by three to six players. The cards are divided into three categories: questions, statements and jokers. The players take turns to draw a card and reading aloud what is written on the card. If someone draws a card with a question, they are given one minute to answer. If someone draws a statement card, they are given one minute to comment on the statement. Subsequently, the other players are given two minutes to make comments regarding the player's answer or comment. These are examples of the questions a player might be faced with:

1. Do you believe that it is acceptable for volunteers and the users of the organization to also associate with each other in private?
2. What creates personal development among volunteers in your organization?
3. Is it acceptable to present volunteers with specific requirements such as a particular background or specific experience from paid work? and
4. What would it mean if your organization appointed one or several managers with the responsibility of drawing up guidelines for voluntary work?

Characteristic of these questions is, first of all, their focus on the perception among volunteers of the boundary between volunteer and organization. The first question addresses the issue of whether the volunteer even perceives the social relations that are established through the voluntary organization as different from private social relations. That is, does the volunteer consider the organization a space of commitment? The second question concerns the volunteer's inclusion in the organization. The last two questions concern whether or not it is acceptable for a voluntary organization to make formal demands on its volunteers, including the extent to which volunteers accept workplace-like conditions in their work. All the questions are asked from the perspective of organizational management. The person reading from the cards activates the voice of the manager. Questions are asked. Particular questions become lodged into the interaction of the volunteers, but the one posing the questions, the management, is rendered invisible and has been substituted for a stack of playing cards. These cards actualize a specific horizon of questioning. It is not simply a question, but a question that must be answered in order for the players to proceed with the game. An answer is required, but the person who asks the questions does not listen to the answer because the real answer is the question, that is, the notion that the volunteers view themselves, each other, and the organization from the perspective of a specific horizon of questions:

These are some of the statement cards:

1. It is the manager's responsibility to determine which tasks the individual volunteer may take on.
2. The volunteers themselves should define the rules for the volunteer group and its work.
3. Being a volunteer primarily requires empathy and human experience. These should be the only requirements an organization asks of its volunteers.
4. All volunteers should sign a written volunteer contract with the organization.
5. It is problematic if the organization lays down rules for the voluntary work which cannot be enforced.

Again, the cards activate the voice of management, no longer as questions but as statements on the so-called statement cards. These statements scan across possible end points for the relationship between volunteer and organization. Whereas the questions appeal to a notion of positive and shared reflection, the statement cards invite positions of opposition and protest. The cards offer the possibility to formulate a language of opposition. The statements play with and pivot around a 'no' and at the same time seek to control and explicate the horizon of opposition for the volunteers.

The statement cards may look like those shown in Figure 4.1.

What the game 'Attitudes towards volunteer policies' does, in effect, is to establish a space in which the volunteers are invited to play with their understanding of their boundaries vis-à-vis the voluntary organization, the user and each other. The volunteers are

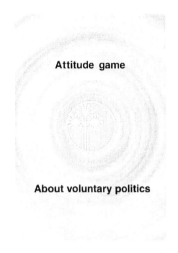

Attitude game

About voluntary politics

Card no. 18
Read the card aloud. Make your statement.
Ask the group about their attitudes.

**Volunteers who cannot observe
the accepted rules are not
useful as volunteers.**

Figure 4.1   A statement card (from Centre for Voluntary Work 2005)

encouraged, in the form of play, to reflect upon dilemmas in voluntary work and to commit voluntarily to specific attitudes towards these questions.

Values at play

The second game, 'Values at play', is also produced by the Centre for Voluntary Social Work. It came out in 2002 and my copy of the game is in the third edition, which suggests that the game is actually being used. The game resembles a family board game. It consists of a board with a number of successive fields laid out in the shape of a circle. The different figures have different shapes and have different names written on them. I will return to this a little later. In addition, there are four plastic pieces of various colours, a die, and six stacks of cards. These stacks of cards each have a name: Peter Pop, Mary Morality, Petra Provo, John Justice, David Dreamer, and Emma Dilemma. All the cards are decorated with colourful drawings of the figures they represent (see Figure 4.2). The objective of the game is to collect a set of cards. The player who is the first to collect one of each kind of card is the winner. Thus, this game allows winning, and the very form of the game suggests that this is a game with a competitive edge.

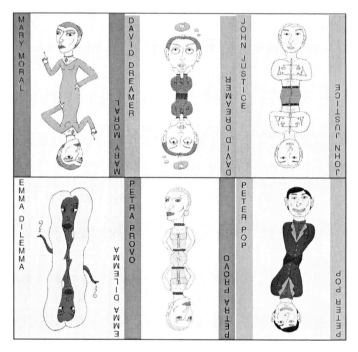

Figure 4.2   Volunteer types (from Centre for Voluntary Work 2002)
Note: Names adapted from Danish: Mary Morality; David Dreamer; John Justice; Peter Pop; Emma Dilemma; and Petra Provo.

Moreover, this games stands out from the other games by making its objective known explicitly in the introduction to the game, which also explains the rules of the game. The objective of the game is described like this: ' "Values at Play" is intended for use in voluntary social organizations. The game can be played by members, volunteers and employees who wish to debate their view of human nature and personal values in the voluntary work they do. The objective of the game is to create reflexivity and awareness about the basis for the attitudes and actions of each player. Through conversation and debate, the game focuses on the relationship between the individual volunteer and other volunteers, users and the local community. There are no right or wrong answers in the game since the objective of the game is to gain insight into oneself and others' (Centre for Voluntary Social Work 2002, own translation).

This description articulates a number of boundaries, that is, the boundaries volunteer/volunteer, volunteer/user and volunteer/local community. It is a multiplication of the boundary volunteer/organization, which is in itself interesting. However, the most interesting aspect of the description is the notion that the boundaries of the voluntary organization are identical to the boundaries of the individual volunteer. This implies that the boundaries between organization and its users equal the sum of the boundaries between the individual and the users. The notion that the volunteer/volunteer, volunteer/user, and volunteer/ local community relationship could be mediated across organizational decisions seems to have been fully suppressed.

Let us take a closer look at the cards. Each time a player lands on a field, he or she draws a card that matches the figure of that field. If a player lands on Emma Dilemma, the player draws an Emma Dilemma card. The player reads the first question on the card and answers the question. Then the other players comment on, debate, or ask questions about the player's answer so that the game continues to regulate the conversation topics throughout the game. The different figures represent six different types of volunteers. Thus, they do not simply represent arbitrary names but actual types that can often be found in voluntary organizations, and which it is fair to presume is present in the form of one or more players at the table. In that way, the questions on the card give voice to the different volunteer types and the different players in the game. We might say that the game expresses a form of orchestrated polyphony with the whole game playing with the idea that the player uses, in different capacities, the voices that the cards represent. The purpose of having each player collect different cards and thus answer different questions is to create a context in which the imagined players answer questions that express different and possibly opposing voices, which are typically found in voluntary organizations. In that way, the players are given a chance to see the world from different perspectives, which typically (according to the theory of the game) can be found in their organization.

If we take a look at the questions, they clearly represent different voices. John Justice's questions, for example, represent the voices of law and justice. Modern law has long since placed the question of justice outside the door in the sense that legal courts, for example, make judgments about who is right and wrong in relation to existing legislation while knowing that its judgment does not necessarily coincide with justice. To John Justice, law and justice partially coincide; his voice is not the voice of a professional lawyer but the emphasis is still on formal justice. Here are a few examples of the questions on the cards:

- John just wants to know whether your organization sees volunteers and users as equals? How does this manifest itself in daily life?
- Denmark has laws that regulate many aspects of our social and private lives. Do any of the participants believe that there are some laws that it is acceptable to violate as a volunteer?
- John Justice believes strongly in democracy and the rules it is based on even though it can sometimes take time to change things through the official channels. He wants to know which means you believe that it is okay for your organization to employ in order to change society?
- John Justice greatly appreciates the Danish freedom of association. Do you believe that anyone should be entitled to join your association? Are there persons that they do not accept as members?

John Justice asks questions about the establishment of the boundaries between volunteer/user, law/justice, voluntary organization/society and volunteer/volunteer. And these boundaries are constantly implied and played down as formal boundaries. There are distinctions between right and wrong and it is the right and wrong of the law, which is constantly put at stake.

David Dreamer, in turn, represents the more spiritual and emotional type. His questions sound like this:

- David Dreamer's ideal society is one in which citizens help each other in difficult situations and represent each other's strength. Does your voluntary work in your organization contribute towards this kind of society?
- David Dreamer is convinced that there is more to life *than meets the eye*. He spends a lot of time reading about his star sign in magazines, and he once had someone read his fortune. David Dreamer also believes that his organization should have someone read its fortune for its future work. How do you feel about this idea? Why?

- David Dreamer wants to know what you personally would like to be remembered for in your organization if you had to unexpectedly stop working as a volunteer tomorrow?

Again, these questions focus on boundaries, but from a more naïve and neo-religious position focusing on personal and spiritual development. That means that the boundary between volunteer/society is presumed to be defined not in formal term, but spiritually. Here, it is the spiritual community of solidarity that makes up a voluntary organization, and the relation between volunteer and organization becomes a question, therefore, about whether the organization represents a space within which the volunteer may grow and feel that he or she does some good.

Mary Morality obviously represents the voice of morality and asks questions such as:

- Mary Morality is good at keeping a secret. She believes that it is the responsibility of a volunteer to keep quiet if a promise has been made not to tell something. Do you agree with Mary Morality? Would there be any exceptions?
- Mary Morality believes that she has been raised well, that she brings many life experiences to the organization, and that she has learned a lot in the past 2 years. Is it okay for her to offer advice to people who ask for help, and help them to tell right from wrong?

These questions join the voluntary organization together by virtue of a kind of moral code, and the boundary volunteer/user is a moral boundary concerning right and wrong and the forms of behaviour that should be respected or not.

Peter Pop's approach is energy and high spirits. Some of his questions are:

- Peter Pop really likes working as a volunteer at the local drop-in centre because he has made a lot of new friends among the other volunteers. He enjoys the sense of community and likes to go out after work. Peter Pop asks what you hope to get out of working as a volunteer?
- Peter Pop believes that it is important that volunteers should be able to come and go in the organization depending on their available time and energy. He feels that the organization should not

make too many demands on the volunteer's work and conduct – since that would mean that nobody would want to work there. Which demands do you believe should be made on volunteers?

These questions suggest an understanding of the voluntary organization as almost familial or as an intimate network of friends that is held together by love and the desire to be together. And friendships do not grow out of demands. Here, the voluntary organization is not allowed to come through as an organization.

The different cards clearly represent different approaches, and the game makes it possible to set these up against each other. It encourages polyphony without presenting any right answers. The six types represent different voices of value in the voluntary organization, but at the same time a volunteer is not inclined to fully identify with any of the voices. The voices do not work as complete representatives for the different types of volunteers. Rather, they are mild parodies of types of volunteers. These parodies function in a way so that the players are forced to approach the questions and statements with a certain distance. It has clearly been the intent to produce a value game that did not presume that there is a right answer. The game provides possibilities for reflections but not for identity and a specific standpoint. None of the types represent a hero in the game. The game signals that it takes the players' discussions seriously by not suggesting that a player may guess what the designer of the game considers the right answer and positions. The result, however, is a partial ridiculing of the volunteer. 'Values at play' is a fun game about serious values, but it becomes almost too much fun and lacks any real space for independent reflection. Nobody wants to identify completely with Peter Pop or any of the other characters, and there exists no seventh position aside from that of reflection. However, when this position is posited as a reflection upon voices that are made the object of parody, it becomes difficult for it to represent an alternative to these.

Like 'Attitudes towards volunteer policies', this game is about encouraging the volunteer to create and reflect upon boundaries concerning voluntary work. Unlike the first game, however, this game provides an additional level of reflection because it defines the dilemmas of volunteer work as dependent upon perspective. Dilemmas becomes polycontextual; their character depends on the 'voice' that speaks and observes them, that is to say, the voices of morality, law, spirituality, love and friendship. In any case, the organization has withdrawn as the producer of decision premises. The organization does not establish its boundaries through decision but encourages the volunteers to play forth its boundaries. The volunteers are invited to a personal commitment with respect to the boundaries and positions they play into existence. Playing is a voluntary act, but if one plays, one commits oneself. But it is not only the volunteers that are thus placed in a paradoxical situation. The organization places itself in a similar situation. The organization, as it is, pulls back in its role as premise creator and encourages its members to play games with its boundaries, but do these games not also commit the organization itself? Thus, the organization finds itself in a paradoxical situation in which it has to oscillate between taking the volunteers' games seriously, on one hand, and at the same time maintaining the position that this was precisely play and games, which does not bind the organization.

2. The school/family boundary

The following two games, 'Short and sweet in the family' and 'The game of responsibility', each in their own way put the boundary between family and school into play. Both games show the way in which the organization of games is used to establish boundaries and the delegation of responsibilities. However, the two games also represent two very different strategies for playing with the same boundary. The first game describes itself as a social-pedagogical game and is intended to be played, like a Trojan horse, in the home by an individual family. The game is publicly ordained but is played in private. Through the game, the family is encouraged to articulate the family members' mutual relations, including the parents' support or lack of support of the child's school relationship. The nature of the game is therapeutic. The second game takes place in public but establishes private commitment. The game is a dialogue game through which parents exchange attitudes towards the placement of responsibility between school and the home in relation to different tasks. The game professes to be about making different expectations to school, home, and the relationship between them visible, but it ends up by suddenly being reified as decision.

We have witnessed great changes in state schools in recent years, which have contributed to challenge the boundary between school and family (the following section is based on work done by Hanne Knudsen who is currently writing her PhD dissertation about state school management with a focus on the relationship between school and home (Knudsen 2007, 2008). The boundary between school and family has always been problematic and has always included a dispute about 'ownership' of the children Therefore, the schools have always had to define a boundary in relation to the families. This boundary has primarily been formal and has been defined through laws about compulsory school attendance, which were then to be further explicated by the individual school. In addition, since the early 1900s the school has been interested in the family as a premise for education based on the notion that parents' background and their childrearing methods represent significant factors in determining what type of learning can take place in the classroom. In the post-war years, cooperation with parents became institutionalized, for example in the form of parent-teacher consultations, which serves the purpose of informing parents of their children's progress and thus support and underpin the learning that takes place within the family such as homework help and supervision. Over the past 20 years the state school has shifted away from single-subject programmes towards a cross-curricular programme, and at the same time learning has shifted in the direction of second-order learning. Knowledge is no longer considered to have durability over time. Therefore, it does not suffice for children to learn a great deal. They have to primarily learn to learn, which also entails learning to see themselves from a learning perspective. This is often referred to as 'being responsible for own learning'. This means that the state schools develop a greater sensitivity towards other types of competencies than strictly subject ones. Social and personal competencies become central to teaching. This has different implications. First of all, it means a much more differentiated concept of pedagogy in state schools, where traditional teacher-controlled classroom teaching gives way to group work, projects, personal presentations, and cooperation across classes, grades, and subjects. The new forms are intended to support the students' personal and social development, but paradoxically they presuppose a great number of personal and social competences in order to be effective. The students are no longer simply expected to be disciplined. They must learn the different rules that apply in different teaching methods. Sometimes they are expected to act as quiet listeners; other times they need to be engaged and involved, and still other times to work together. This means that they need to be able to oscillate between many different student roles. And it also means that the family's socialization of the children comes to play a much greater role. The school becomes more dependent upon the families' ability to provide students to the school with a much more differentiated level of socialization; children who are able to do a lot more than simply sit still. Today's state school describes itself like this: 'The responsibility of the public school [state school in the UK] is to work together with parents to further the student's acquisition of knowledge, abilities, work methods, and forms of expression, which contribute to the versatile personal development of the individual student'. The school develops an interest for the families' internal creation of themselves as families. The responsibility of the families in relation to the school is displaced from specific responsibilities, such as making sure that the children attend school and ensuring that their homework gets done, towards the creation of the family as a sound space of development and learning for the children. It is not only the children who are expected to relate to themselves pedagogically. The family has to do the same. However, this creates a problem for the school because it develops a management ambition in relation to a system (the family), which fundamentally resides outside the formal domain of the school. Some ways to deal with this problem has been a growing involvement of parents in school boards, more parent-teacher meetings, and an effort to transform parent meetings from informational meetings to dialogue-based meetings. One of the currently popular phrases is 'partnerships between school and home'. This is where the concept of play is introduced once again. The schools begin to develop games for the purpose of regulating the processes through which the families define themselves and their boundary and responsibility vis-à-vis the school; processes in relation to which they have absolutely no formal decision competency.

I am going to analyse two games, which in very different ways express the schools' effort to regulate the family's creation of boundaries in relation to the school. The first game is called 'Short and sweet in the family' and is intended for use at home by the individual family. The school provides the family with the game. The second game,

'The game of responsibility', is designed to take place at the school and to include many parents at the same time.

Short and sweet in the family

'Short and sweet in the family' is one game in a series of games. Some of these are entitled: 'Short and sweet in introductory education', 'Short and sweet: Grades 3–6', 'Short and sweet: Grades 7–10', and 'Honestly I: A game of conversation for parent meetings grades K-5'. The series also includes a video from 1996 entitled 'Ebbe receives the yellow card', which demonstrates, with examples from a classroom, the way in which the game is and should be used. The entire series is designed by Carl Olav Hansen. Some editions of 'Short and sweet' are used widely in Danish public schools and some of the games have been purchased by 70 percent of all public schools in Denmark.

The 'Short and sweet' series has been studied by Klaus Nielsen as expressing a confessional figure. He sees 'Short and sweet' as the indication of a shift in the techniques for disciplining: 'Whereas disruption and trouble was disciplined through corporal punishment 50 years ago, today's students are disciplined by means of therapeutic confessional techniques' (Nielsen 2005: 82, own translation). In short, according to Nielsen, it is a question of 'allowing the student to take over the disciplining function in relation to each other and particularly in relation to themselves' (Nielsen 2005: 82, own translation). I am going to leave this line of thinking untouched and only consider the way in which these games present themselves and in particular the way in which they are presented precisely as games and play.

The games all share in common the description of them as social-pedagogical conversation games using cards (and sometimes also dice) as the primary medium. The individual game typically consists of a number of happy cards and unhappy cards. When a player roles the die and gets a specific number, he or she draws a card. The player reads from the card and then has to pass the card on to one of the other players that the first player believes the card to represent. In the game 'Short and Sweet in introductory education', for example, a happy statement could be 'I pay attention to your actions'. An unhappy card could read 'You often disrupt class when we sit in a circle'. Each card begins a conversation, which is structured somewhat differently in the different games depending on considerations such as age. In most of the games, the classroom teacher is assigned the role of game master who has the right to raise question that might guide the conversation along. A question could be: 'Why do you think you were given this card by xxx?' The game material mentions this question as an example. Once all the cards have been dealt, there is a so-called re-working of the game. Not all players have necessarily received a card and there might be an uneven distribution of happy and unhappy cards. The game guide stresses the fact that the game is a 'conversation game in which everyone is a winner' (from the introductory education game). However, even if everyone wins, some of the players probably perceive and express themselves more as winners than others. Therefore, the re-working of the game raises questions such as 'How did it feel to receive this card?', 'Do you feel that the cards were distributed in an appropriate way?', and 'Did anyone feel like gaining revenge when they received a bad card?' A few of the cards from the introductory education game are shown below (Figure 4.3).

I am going to now focus on the family game. The game is subtitled 'A social-pedagogical game for the family'. On the front cover of the game rule booklet is a drawing of a nuclear family consisting of a father, a mother, a son and a daughter. They are depicted sitting on and around the family's couch – that is, not in the kitchen and not at

Figure 4.3 Short and sweet in school, a social pedagogical game (from Hansen 1997d)

the dining room table, but in the section of the house that most often denotes comfort and relaxation. Father and mother are sitting on the couch and on the wall behind them are painted landscape motifs. The brother and sister are sitting on a stool and a beanbag respectively. The father has a friendly beard. He is wearing a turtleneck sweater and no shoes. On the table in the middle are dice cups, dice and cards. They are clearly enjoying themselves. They are smiling and look relaxed. They represent normality itself. The text underneath the drawing reads: 'The game that gives the family something to talk about'. The style of the drawing is naïve and child-like, like children's books illustrations. The game is clearly presented as a game, which, like Sorry or Yatzy, is played by the family in a relaxed atmosphere with no other purpose than the enjoyment of playing. But at the same time, the game gives the family something to talk about.

Unlike Sorry or Yahtzee however, the family does not purchase the game from the local toy store or bookstore. The game, which comes in a little blue cardboard box, indicates kinship with other educational material. The game is produced by Special-pædagogisk forlag (a special-pedagogical publishing house), and it finds its way into the family through a teacher in the children's school. It is a game that a family is selected to play. Not everyone gets it. It is a game that the teacher gives to the family to take home if he or she believes that the family needs it and may learn from it. However, this aspect is not mentioned anywhere in the game material. The booklet that comes with the game simply tells us (1) what the game includes, that is, a description of the cards in the game, (2) things needed to play the game (dice cup and two dice), (3) rules of the game, and (4) questions for reworking when the game is over. The material never mentions what the game expects from the family. It does not indicate an objective outside the game, which would define the game as a task. There are no social-pedagogical descriptions of the way the game works. All we have is the brief indication on the front page of the booklet: 'A social-pedagogical game for the family'.

The reason that I focus on the family game is that it does not take place at school but in the family. It is ordained by the school but is played solely and completely by the family itself. Thus, the game functions as particular medium that the school can employ in relation to the family. The family represents the school's environment, and the school is equipped with very limited authority vis-à-vis the family. Where authority ends is where the game seems to take over. The school can offer the family something as innocent as a game; a game that presents itself as a game like any other game – and it even provides topics for conversation.

Let us take a closer look at what these topics for conversation are. There are three types of cards – yellow, grey, and blue – and a specific role of the dice means that the player gets to draw a card, read it out loud, and give it to the person it fits. The player may also give the card to herself. If the card does not, in the player's opinion, fit any of the players, the card is returned to the stack. If the player decides to give the card to someone, he or she must explain the way in which the card fits that person. Some of the yellow cards – also called sceptical cards – read: 'You are rarely there when I need you', 'You don't care enough about my work (school)', 'This place would be nicer if you were more happy', 'You rarely give praise', 'I often don't know why when you are upset'. The grey cards are intended as positive and appreciative cards. Some of them read: 'Sometimes I am not sure what you think of me', 'It would be nice if you could be around more', 'I think you care about me a lot', 'It *means* a lot to me that you are happy', 'I like playing with you', 'You never let me down'. These cards are considered to be positive and easy to give to each other in the context of a comfortable game situation. The game communicates expectations about the ability of the son to make these statements to his father or mother; and moreover, that these statements can be made between the children and under the supervision of the parents. Last but not least, the game produces expectations about the ability for the father, mother, son, or daughter to accept these statements in the positive spirit of the game. In addition, the individual cards produce specific expectations. That applies not only to the yellow sceptical cards but also to the grey cards. Statements such as 'It means a lot to me that you are happy', 'I like playing with you', and 'You never let me down' do not simply signal praise. They also communicate ultimate expectations, expectations about *being* happy, *being* prepared to play, and never letting someone down. The statements do not simply state a fact. They also function as prescriptive. Thus, the statements articulate both expectations concerning a present condition but also expectations concerning a future condition. However, statements also always have a hidden side reflecting what could have been said. In communication, there is always a surplus of possibilities for carrying on the communication. So much

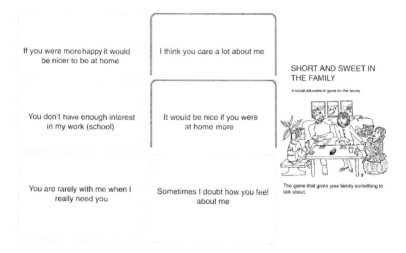

If you were more happy it would
be nicer to be at home

I think you care a lot about me

You don't have enough interest
in my work (school)

It would be nice if you were
at home more

You are rarely with me when I
really need you

Sometimes I doubt how you feel
about me

SHORT AND SWEET IN
THE FAMILY

A social-educational game for the family

The game that gives your family something to
talk about.

Figure 4.4   Short and sweet in the family (from Hansen 1997c)

could be said and in fact so little is said. Saying 'you never let me down' simultaneously says that out of all the possible statements I have chosen to say this; and to you. Even though the statement has been picked out of a stack of cards, it is still said and something else could have been said. One might have decided to put the card back and drawn a new one. However, within the logic of the game, if too many cards are returned to the stack, the game does not continue and the players have contributed to its disruption. The game ends. 'This is not a game' is communicated and the comfort of the situation is disrupted. Figure 4.4 shows a few cards and the front page of the game booklet.

As with the other 'Short and sweet in the family games', this game suggests a so-called re-working once all cards have been drawn and distributed. However, unlike the other games, there is no teacher here in the role of game master. There is not a position outside the game, who may take responsibility for the re-working. Therefore, the players have to do the re-working among themselves. The booklet suggests that the players ask 10 questions. These questions may include: 'How did it feel to be given a grey card?', 'What was more specifically on your mind when you gave me this card', 'Were there cards missing?', and 'What would have been written on these?'. On one hand, the fact that these questions are referred to as re-working indicates that the game is over. On the other hand, however, it seems to continue the game to the extent that the questions carry on the conversations of the game. Indicating that the game is over at the same time as it is carried on raises the question whether it was ever really a game.

All in all, 'Short and sweet in the family' encourages the individual family to articulate family members' mutual relationships. It encourages the family to put its self-creation into words. A family has many boundaries. The family members participate in many other communication systems outside the family. They work, go to school, have hobbies, etc., and the game encourages conversation about these systems boundaries, not least whether the family and its individual members are sufficiently tuned to the fact that the children are students in a school with certain responsibilities that affect their family life.

The game of responsibility

'The game of responsibility' is a completely different game produced by the Danish public school system about the relationship between school and family. It is developed by the municipality of Aarhus and is part of a comprehensive programme for cooperation between school and home, published in the collection of material from 2003 entitled *Together we can do more*. Among other things the material includes the core values of the municipality and their policy for school–home cooperation. In addition, it includes a range of tools that the municipal schools are encouraged to use in their approach to the relationship between school and home. These pertain in particular to a number of concepts for evening meetings for parents at the school. Generally speaking, an evening meeting for parents is divided into three parts: welcome; issues; and summing up. Play comes into play already in the welcome part. The material compilation presents five different get-to-know-each-other games in addition to 10 name games, 11 dances, and six songs. Each of these games is about bringing people together in a comfortable and relaxed atmosphere. The issues part of the meeting is designed to address heavier concepts of which the responsibility game is one. Others are questions such as; What do we dream about?, Wishes for my child and Communication: Practice and role play. It is suggested that the event ends up with a song that strikes a lighter tone.

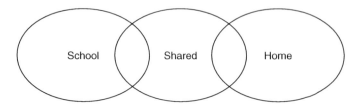

Figure 4.5   Distribution of responsibility

The responsibility game is designed in a way so that it can be easily adjusted both with respect to content and process, which makes it applicable on different grade levels. The objective of the responsibility game is described as making expectations between school and home visible with respect to practical arrangements, emotional relationships and interpersonal relations. Having brought the parents together by means of a dance or a get-to-know-each-other game, the evening's programme is introduced and the parents are divided into groups of four to six. The role of the teachers in most versions of the responsibility game is that of instructors who move around among the groups. Some of the responsibility games that are intended for older grades also include the students. The responsibility game is divided into three rounds. The first round takes place in the individual group seated around a table. On the table is a game board as shown in Figure 4.5.

On the table is also a stack of 32 cards. Each card describes a responsibility in relation to the child. The questions on the cards read: Who is responsible for making sure:

1. That the child is not hungry in school?
2. That the child takes his seat when the bell rings?
3. That the child gets to school – in time?
4. That the child is rested?
5. That the child is organized (pencil box, books, etc.)?
6. That the child is able to actively listen when someone else speaks?
7. That the child understands a collective message and is able to act accordingly?
8. That the child writes down homework in the homework book?
9. That the child learns?
10. That the child plays well during recess?

11. That the child is able to handle conflicts between her/himself and others?
12. That the child remembers to bring home a message?
13. That the child remembers to bring home her possessions?
14. That the child does his homework?
15. That the child helps with cleaning up the classroom before leaving?
16. That the child has some quality free time?
17. That the child likes to go to school?
18. That the child learns that a deal is a deal?
19. That the child learns perseverance in her work?
20. That the child learns to be considerate?
21. That demands made on the child are manageable?
22. That the child feels that 'I am good enough'?
23. That the child is given the sense of being 'seen'?
24. That the child learns to cooperate?
25. That the child develops an understanding of other people's differences?
26. That the child learns to tolerate losing a game?
27. That the child develops her creativity and imagination?
28. That the child experiences happy days?
29. That the child becomes independent?
30. That the child feels safe enough to express his opinions and feelings?
31. That the child becomes a good friend?
32. That the child leans to take responsibility?

During the first round, the parents draw cards from the stack and answer whether the responsibility pertaining to their specific question should be placed in the home, in school, or whether it is a shared responsibility. Then the group discusses the placement of responsibility and the card either remains in the original position or is moved to another field. It is important to explore the possibility for agreement in the group.

The second round focuses on the cards that have been selected as shared responsibility questions. Based on a discussion, the group prioritizes the three most important cards for shared responsibility between school and home. Then the group discusses what the school and the parents respectively can contribute to the cooperation concerning the three selected questions. The questions and considerations are written down on an overhead.

The third round takes place in the plenary session where the groups present their overheads and proposals for a division of responsibility between school and home. Then the instructors type up the overheads and place them in 'The book of cooperation' (Aarhus Municipality School Agency 2003: 2.19–2.23).

We are dealing with a game about responsibility, arranged by the school for the parents and taking place under the auspices of the school. The game explicitly states that it is about boundaries: How to draw the boundary between the responsibility of schools and families? What can be defined as shared responsibility? And what is the school's and family's share respectively of the shared responsibility? The game is introduced as a game of cards and a game board, and the placement of the cards on the board is entirely open and up for discussion. At the same time, however, the school has already defined the total sum of responsibility in advance. The total sum of responsibility represents the rules of the responsibility game. The parents are not given the chance to formulate new cards, and so there is an established limit to the openness. In other words: There are pre-established boundaries for the way in which the boundary between school and home can be defined in the meeting with the parents. The responsibility game is presented to the parents as a game. However, at the end of the game the instructors write up the overheads and post them in the cooperation book. Suddenly play has become a decision. What the parents have played into existence is suddenly perceived by the teachers as a decision process, and the conclusion of the game becomes a decision, which is written down and which the school can then refer back to precisely as a collective decision. What was initially introduced as the objective of the game, that is, to make expectations between school and home *visible*, is suddenly transformed into *established* expectations between school and home. And there is clearly a difference between making visible and establishing. The game is simply used to make decisions about that which the school is otherwise unable to make decisions about. Whether the decision ultimately gets to function as a decision is a different question, which depends on whether the document is actually given a communicative afterlife.

3. The individual/community boundary

The third example of political games that I wish to introduce and which puts boundaries at stake are games organized by the NGO *Right to Play*. I will use this case to show the way in which creation games are employed for purposes of civil society development, for the development of communities and responsible individuals-in-the-community. I will focus in this chapter on state financed NGOs and their organization of games, primarily in third world countries. Their goal is to use games to develop societies.

The NGO *Right to Play* organizes games and sports events in a number of third world countries. These games share in common their link to a specific objective, e.g. health issues or conflict resolution, and they are all concerned with the notion of empowerment, both on a personal level and with respect to the local community. The idea is to play resourceful communities into existence.

Right to Play (2007b) has three main objectives:

- *Holistic Child Development*: *Right to Play* uses sports and play programmes to promote the healthy physical, social and emotional development of children that is essential to the future of healthy communities and the re-building of civil society, on a local and global level.
- *Individual and Community Capacity Building*: Working closely with communities, *Right To Play* assists in the setup of the networks and infrastructure necessary to support sustainable local ownership of sports and play programmes. We also train local youth to be coached imparting leadership skills, and ensuring sustainability of the life skills emphasized by our programme.
- *Social Mobilization to Reduce the Incidence of Disease*: *Right To Play* uses sport and play to mobilize communities around key health issues in a fun and social way specifically to support national health objectives and campaigns'

The organization's programme states: 'Sport and play are also effective tools for mobilizing and educating communities around key health issues. Play provides a positive path to healthy child development. Sport can teach the positive behaviours of leadership, discipline, teamwork and fair play. The development of communities is enhanced when individuals have the capacity to act in ways that lead and build the community. Through a coach-based approach both individuals and their communities can learn valuable skills that will serve as catalysts for community development' (*Right to Play* 2007a).

Right to Play's programme includes five modules. The first is called *Coach2coach* and is designed to create motivating local coaches who can lead and supervise exercise and play with children on a daily basis. *Coach2coach* works to develop the capacity for local individual leadership and community responsibility. The second module is called *Live safe, play safe (LSPS)* and is based on a programme of health pedagogy. Through physical activities and guided discussions, the programme seeks to engage children and adolescents in health-oriented activities. The module contains three key words: *Knowledge*, which refers to the understanding of body and sickness; *Attitude*, which refers to emotions, values, and attitudes towards one's own and other people's lives. It is about self-esteem and confidence; and *skills* which concerns the participants' ability to be responsible for specific practices such as using a condom. The third module is called *Red ball child play*. It is based on a holistic approach to child development and includes a range of games about learning and personal development. These games use five different coloured balls that each denotes different developmental values. Red is a 'mind ball' and represents cognitive and intellectual development. The black ball represents the physical development of children's bodies as well as their awareness and understanding of their own bodies. The yellow ball represents the child's emotional development, including joy, self-esteem, happiness and hope. Green is the health ball, and represents health and wellbeing. Finally, blue is the peace ball representing the social aspects of development, including friendship, family, community, and nature. The fourth module is *Community Infrastructure Capacity Building* and is about establishing local sports NGOs. Finally, the fifth module is *Physical Infrastructure Development*. It is about building basic sports and play grounds (*Right to Play* 2007c).

One example is a game entitled *Infection Protection*. Its aim is to empower children to take responsibility for their own health and hygiene. Through play, the children are to learn to protect themselves against infections. The instructions for the game read:

1. Select one child to be the 'virus,' and another to be the 'body.' The remaining children are the 'immune system'.

2. The children representing the immune system join hands and form a big circle around the body. The virus is on the outside.
3. The virus tries to touch the body, while the immune system moves around to prevent the virus from touching the body. If the virus touches the body, the body gets sick. The virus and body switch places, and a new virus and body continue.
4. The game leader blows the whistle after one minute for the children to switch places if the virus has not yet been touched.
5. After finishing the game, the game leader talks to the children about the role of the immune system in preventing disease, and how getting vaccinated would also help' (Right to play 2007b).

Characteristic of *Right to Play* is the ambition of civil society development and community development. The aim is to develop communities capable of taking responsibility for themselves and for peace, health issues and development. However, the challenge is that communities do not allow themselves to be decided from outside or from above. Play in this context represents both the means and the end. Play in itself is considered a positive thing, a human right, particularly for children, similar to housing, food and education. But play is also a means because it is considered an enabler of community building. Through play, the children are given insight into different issues. At the same time, they become resourceful in relation to specific problems and build experiences with respect to collective problem solution. Play, therefore, is a strategy for collective empowerment in which the individual is not considered a resourceful individual until she partakes in a community. One is only an individual, in *Right to Play*'s conception, together with others. *Right to Play* is a partly state financed NGO working to develop individuals-in-communities. It is a form of politics without a visible political subject where the political takes the form of play.

4. The state/school/family boundary

My final example is a game produced by the National Board of Health and the Danish Veterinary and Food Administration in cooperation with the organization School and Society. I want to use this example to show the way in which games are used to cut across sector boundaries.

Indeed, The National Board of Health and The Ministry for Food, Agriculture and Fisheries use games to act within the realms of The Ministry of Education, thus positioning themselves as a parasite on the family contract of the Danish public schools. Moreover, I will show the way in which games can be organized so that its players are able to freely join the game but are not able to leave it again. The game is simply structured so that it appears to be voluntary to join but proves to be binding if one wishes to leave it.

There have been great changes in both health and food policies over the past 15 years, and these fields have changed from sector policies to horizontal cross-sectoral policies whose regulatory strategies work to make other policies and institutions include health and food concerns in their self-management.

This change has to do with the fact that the central questions can no longer be clearly limited and treated as distinct problems. Whereas food policies prior to World War II concerned scarcity of food, and later scarcity of specific nutrients, today, food policy concerns healthy versus risky life styles. In the past, issues of food policies could be delimited reasonably clearly as specific issues of scarcity, which could be addressed, for example by adding protein to flower. Today, where illnesses and diseases can be connected to what we eat, the problem is not seen as what we eat, because what we eat is perceived in itself as a symptom of a flawed lifestyle that includes food and exercise habits, an individual's perception of 'the good life', etc (Christensen & Andersen 1999). Figure 4.6 shows how the Danish Government's catalogue of ideas for a programme of public health illustrated the problem.

The model indicates the difficulty of delimiting health problems. The health and wellbeing of the individual is perceived as a result of immediate strains on the health such as tobacco, alcohol and nutrition. These, in turn, are linked to particular circumstances such as family, work and lifestyle, which, in turn, are linked to more general living conditions within society: social, economic and cultural relations.

This means that health policies have to be defined horizontally and cross-sectorally. Rather than operating through and within its own institutions, health policy is forced to try to operate through other institutions both private and public. The first time this ambition

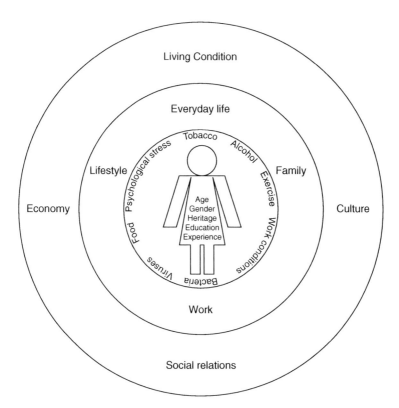

Figure 4.6 Model for health in a social context (from Ministry of Interior and Health (Indenrigs- og Sundhedsministeriet) (2006))

is seriously articulated was in the Danish government's programme for public health in 1999: 'The objective of the programme for public health is to ensure political responsibility for an effective prioritization and coordination of prevention measures across sectors, administrative levels and competencies. We emphasize, therefore, the development of cooperative relations in those areas where today we observe grey zones with respect to responsibility (Ministry of Health 1999: 6, own translation; for a closer analysis of the program, see Højlund & Larsen 2001). The programme points to four so-called

prevention environments through which the programme for public health must operate. These are: primary schools; the workplace;
local communities; and the healthcare system. The programme refers
to the primary schools like this: 'The primary school should provide a health-promoting environment and provide its students with
the basis for promoting their own health and that of others' (Ministry of Health 1999: 8, own translation). The programme for public
health resulted in the establishment of the campaign institution The
National Council on Public Health who writes in one of their many
pamphlets: 'The central issue in health promotion is that the individual has to learn to master her existence, and we, the public authorities,
must help create the best possible circumstances. Mastering one's life
is not always a private matter' (National Council on Public Health
2002: 11, own translation).

Health at play

In 2007, together with the organization School and Society, The
National Board of Health and the Danish Veterinary and Food Administration published the game *Health at play – dialogue and cooperation
about health in the school.*

The purpose of the game is to initiate dialogue about health in
schools and to formulate and agree on issues of food and meals,
movement, drugs, wellbeing, knowledge and attitudes.

The game is based on a rather ambitious health ideal that intervenes
in almost all aspects of life. The game refers to this ideal as a 'positive
concept of health' defined in opposition to other conceptions, which
merely concern the prevention of sickness. Health is said to concern
lifestyle (how we choose to live our lives including eating and exercise habits), *living conditions* (the framework within which we are able
to choose including work and housing), *quality of life* (what makes us
feel happy), *physical wellbeing* (feeling good about and within our bodies), *psychological wellbeing* (feeling good about our mental condition,
including self-esteem), and *social wellbeing* (our ability to partake in a
communal space, including making friends). This definition of health
leaves no aspect of life to be defined outside the domain of health policy. Life in all its facets becomes a health concern. The introduction
to the game says: 'All these areas represent important elements of a
healthy life and are of equal importance in the dialogue'.

The game comes with a short presentation video, which can also be found on the National Board of Health's website. The video includes interviews with different stakeholders about the game. In the video, health consultant for Gladsaxe Municipality, Teresa Dominicussen, says: 'As a municipality, we could simply and single-handedly define the framework for defining health, but it is important that both parents and students are able to recognize themselves so that it is not only something they engage in while in school but something they carry over into their lives at home'. The video then goes directly to Karsten Jensen, a consultant, who says: 'The question is not whether we should all live the same way; whether we should all have the same preferences. In a diverse society, it is important that there is room for differences' (Danish Veterinary and Food Administration, National Board of Health and School and Society 2007). This is the regulation problem in a nutshell, which is what *Health at Play* is supposed to provide a response to. There is a wish to regulate what takes place in the home so that home activities can be perceived as healthy. At the same time, however, it is not possible to articulate this regulatory ambition without violating the boundary between private and public, which is also the boundary of public regulation. Regulating through play enables the public authorities to have their cake and also eat it by simultaneously asserting the regulatory ambition concerning the private while also asserting the respect for the autonomy of private life.

Health at Play is intended for use in the context of parent events, pedagogy days, or events for older students. It takes approximately 2 hours to play. The game is instructed by a teacher and is set up by dividing parents into groups of four to six seated at different tables. On each table is placed a game board with three spaces entitled 'agree', 'partially agree', and 'disagree'. Clearly, the agenda is about regulating consensus. Each of the groups is given a stack of statements. Some of these are:

- It is not okay for students to try alcohol at home.
- Movement and play need to be incorporated into more classes than just physical education.
- Students need knowledge, experience, and positive role models in order to choose healthy alternatives to soft drinks, candy and chips.
- Parents are the children's most important role models.

- Parents are responsible for establishing a strong parent network in the class.
- Children and young people need to be motivated to live a healthy lifestyle.
- Children and young people must learn to take responsibility for their own health.

The game instructions outline a structure for the course of the dialogue. There are six phases of the game. During the first phase, the groups discuss the statements and reach consensus about which statements they agree with, disagree with, or partially agree with. In this way, the statement cards are placed on the different squares of the game board. During the second phase, the group focuses on the statement cards that the group agrees with. The group selects three statements, which they believe are the most relevant as the basis of establishing agreements. The three statements are given a priority from one to three. During the third phase, the groups are handed a prioritization table (shown in Figure 4.7) and have to come up with suggestions for action for parents, students and the school respectively in response to the individual statements. These suggestions are written down. During the fourth phase, the groups present their suggestions to each other. There is no discussion. During the fifth phase, the groups' suggestions for actions are suddenly referred to as suggestions for agreements, and the groups are encouraged to discuss which of the suggested agreements could apply to the class as a whole. During the sixth phase, the instructor sums up the selected statements and collective agreements in a prioritization table, which is subsequently emailed to all participants 'so that we all know which agreements have been reached'. The instructor suggests that the collective agreements should be evaluated at subsequent parent meetings.

One might question whether this qualifies as play. It is called a game, but it ends up as agreements. It is also called dialogue, but the communication is carefully planned both socially in terms of who can play and when, factually with respect to which statements to discuss, and temporally in terms of the communication's sequential division into phases. The game is described as a game – not as a decision process, but its structure is similar to very formal decision structures. The game does not convey the fact that its aim is health agreements. These agreements are slipped in through the back

PRIORITIZATION TABLE   **HEALTH AT PLAY**

FRUIT WATER *VEGETABLES* EXERCISE PLAY *055150265* RESPONSIBILITY *SELF-CONFIDENCE* LIGHT DRIVE *CLASSROOM* FRIENDSHIP *HAPPINESS* TRUST *AIR*

	Prioritized statements	Suggested arrangements for parents	Suggested arrangements for pupils	Suggested initiatives for the schools/the management
1				
2				
3				

Figure 4.7 Prioritization table (from Danish Veterinary and Food Administration (Fødevarestyrelsen), National Board of Health (Sundhedsstyrelsen) and School and Society (Skole og Samfund) (2007): *Sundhed på spil – dialog og samarbejde om klassens sundhead*, Copenhagen)

door, and the game never encourages dialogue about whether agreements should be made in the first place. One could argue that it is a game in the sense that the reached agreements have been created in a way so that the communicative afterlife of the agreements obtains an oscillating quality, constantly oscillating between observations of the agreements as agreements and observations of the agreements as an agreement game.

On the level of play, parents and the school are parties in the agreement facing each other as independent legal actors with the possibility of binding their own freedom. The game refers to 'collective agreements', which can be reached together with parents as if they were one body or at least one collective legal actor rather than separate individuals. But the parents are not a collective body. That is a fiction within the game, a fiction that nonetheless is used as a power technology in relation to the individual parent who appears to be disloyal if he refuses to play the game. The whole game is based on the expectation that no individual parent is going to refuse to be part of the game. And why would any parent do so as long as it is simply a game? So everyone plays only to discover that the game is not a game but a negotiation and decision process. However, one is still unable to refuse to play because as soon as one says no, the negotiation process is going to return to simply being a game, and as part of a game there is no possibility for the parents' opinions to play a binding role. The game therefore produces the peculiar situation that it is impossible to exit the game even though one has voluntarily entered into it. And if one says no, one no longer wants to play, and whoever does not want to play does not makes a good playmate. Moreover, articulating the negotiation and decision process as a game or as play is a way of getting around the difficulty that the agreement cannot be sanctioned. Parent meetings are not an organization where parents are authorized to makes binding decisions. Therefore, the school pretends to makes collective decisions and emphasizes throughout the game the impression of consensus among parents, which it will subsequently be difficult for individual parents to deviate from.

Another interesting aspect of the agreements is that they do not only define specific obligations. In fact, the collective agreements outline obligations with respect to the self-creation of the families. The families commit to creating themselves in the image of a healthy family. Thus, the collective agreements mean not only a commitment of one's individual freedom. It is also a commitment to a specific way of creating oneself as a free family. Therefore, one is not free until one has created oneself and one's family in a way so that one's lifestyle, living conditions, quality of life, physical well-being, and social well-being can be considered healthy (for the contractualization of the citizen: Andersen 2003, 2004b, 2007a, 2008b).

It is important to note that it is not the Ministry of Education who is originator of the game. The game is distributed by The National Board of Health and The Ministry for Food, Agriculture and Fisheries, who have entered into an agreement with the private organization School and Society about distribution of the game. Thus, The National Board of Health and The Ministry for Food, Agriculture and Fisheries use the health game to reach out to institutions outside their administrative jurisdiction. The National Board of Health and The Ministry for Food, Agriculture and Fisheries hold no authority in relation to the public schools. With the cooperation with the organization School and Society, The National Board of Health and The Ministry for Food, Agriculture and Fisheries attempt to make the game appear as a product from within the school system. As it is, The National

Board of Health and The Ministry for Food, Agriculture and Fisheries do not have many interfaces with different types of citizens. They in particular have no contact to families. Families represent systems outside the control and regulatory embrace of The National Board of Health and The Ministry for Food, Agriculture and Fisheries. With the health game, they basically seek to become parasites on the parent–school cooperation of the public schools by skimming a potential regulatory surplus in the public schools' parent-school cooperation for school-promoting purposes by trying to make them appear as purposes from within the school system. As we saw it in a few of the examples from the schools, school–home cooperation is considered a major challenge which is why The Ministry of Education as well as many municipalities and public schools are heavily engaged in the development of new concepts, policies and institutions for such cooperation. With the health game The National Board of Health and The Ministry for Food, Agriculture and Fisheries play on the current demand for alternative ways of structuring school–home cooperation.

5. Conclusion

In this chapter, I have focused on political games because they demonstrate in the most radical way the way in which games can organize play in relation to boundaries. As we have seen, a range of new political creation games puts different constitutive boundaries at stake, such as school/family and individual/collective. There are both similarities and differences in their ways of doing so. However, what the games have in common is the fact that they move the definition of boundaries away from general decisions and onto the interaction with those involved, where the definition of boundaries is no longer tied to the organizational premise machine.

Generally, the boundaries of the constitutional state are seen as universal. If citizens are protected by rights, all citizens are protected. The law's definition of boundaries between citizen and authorities defines the boundaries as beyond discussion. This is precisely what constitutes their nature of boundary. Boundaries represent second-order rules: rules for the creation of rules. The boundaries constitute the framework for possible interaction, for example, between citizen and authorities, and thus define invariable rules for what can be part of the interaction and how. However, in games, these boundaries seem to have been rendered particular, fluid and personal, and one might therefore rightfully ask whether the boundaries that the games concern can even be perceived as boundaries. At the same time, they do in a sense have the boundaries' status of rules of a higher order. The games pertain to boundaries for relations. They are games about games and games about which game rules should pertain to the relationship, for example, between school and family.

The definition of boundaries renders the boundaries particular in the sense that they are not defined by means of generally applicable decisions. By contrast, different groups such as parent and teacher groups may agree on different boundaries for the school–home cooperation. Thus, the boundaries become particular in relation to specific systems of interactions and the same applies to their validity.

Moreover, boundaries become fluid. When boundaries are defined as something that is played into existence, they do not become established once and for all as applicable to everyone. They can always become the object of further play. They are always preliminary. If we define boundaries as the framing of relations and the definition of game rules, that is, as delimitation of expectations with respect to expectations in specific relational communication contexts such as for example cooperation between schools and homes, then it makes a difference that the boundary is not formal but played into existence. It is precisely a boundary that is at once binding and non-binding for the cooperation: that is, they become boundaries and not-boundaries at the same time. Expectations with respect to expectations are played into existence so that the communication can always become displaced to a meta-level if the communication moves in the direction of conflict. When that happens, one can always say that it was just a game.

Finally, the boundaries seem to have become personalized. All boundary games emphasize personal engagement and personal responsibility in relation to the formulation of the boundary. Therefore, boundaries obtain the character not of an external objectively calculable rule but of an internal sense of commitment in the involved persons.

When boundaries are rendered tied through interaction to creation games, strategy becomes immanent in the games. Creation games seem to be functionally equivalent with the strategic form of reality of the polycentric administration in which the perspective on the world always includes a strategic choice. That is: problems are always problems-in-perspectives, time is a strategic formation of expectations, and communities are established, chosen and opted out of continually, and the choice of community also entails the choice of different distinctions between us and them, between we who take responsibility and the others who do not. Creation games are a way for the administration to seek to influence the self-creation of its environment. Thus, it is not just a possibility to impact the environment but a possibility to shape the way in which systems in the environment create themselves, e.g. the way in which the family or the citizen may render themselves relevant in a particular way to the environment for the school. Thus, creation games unite strategy and play in a challenge to create an environment that renders the citizen relevant. In other words, it is my job to make sure someone wants to play with me. That is precisely the challenge for the National Board of Health and the Ministry for Food, Agriculture and Fisheries: to make families, school and students perceive health as relevant and to make the family play the game. There are not many alternatives when there is no relationship of subordination in relation to the object of regulation. Or defined in terms of strategy: Here, play is the answer to the challenge that the regulatory intention cannot assert itself outside being asserted by the objects of regulation.

In creation games, observed as organizations, membership is privatized. The individual participant has to assume membership. Moreover, the continuation of the game requires that its participants make an active choice to continue to play. And the potential horizon of expectations that the game establishes functions only by virtue of dedication to the game. The result is what we might refer to as the *productive obscurity* of creation games. Not only are a number of expectations produced in the games many, but also the possible status of the expectations. Nobody really knows for sure whether they are taking part in a decision making process, a contract negotiation, a therapeutically treatment, a power struggle of the internal social hierarchy or just a game. So what is agreed about in play, might just be play or an agreement or a decision. There is no way to be certain of the status of the communication. The state is one of heterogeneous undecidability and this obscurity is productive because an eventual resistance to decision making, treatment or contracting is cancelled by the frame of play. The communication can continue in so many different new streams and oscillate between many forms of communication without fixation.

One the other side, political creation games risk expression in a double bound or even triple bound communication. The games seek to unite two or more irreconcilable messages because of the simultaneous heterogeneous forms of communication. In one message, the content is always play. In the other message, the content varies slightly. The 'Game of responsibility' instils play on one hand and decision on the other. 'Values at play' instils play on one hand and reflective self-development on the other. 'Health at play' instils play on one hand and collective agreements on the other. On one hand, 'Short and sweet encourages play'. On the other hand, it is also pedagogical therapy. And at the same time subordination might be the game when a child gives a card to another child saying 'I want to play more together with you'. It puts the participants in a situation where they have to respond to different contradictory packages of expectation at the same time. We know from Bateson what kind of pathological forms of communication which might result from double bound communication (Bateson 2000; see also Cronen, Johnson & Lannamann 1982, Blekinsopp 2007).

Generally, the games are presented on the game's inside, that is, with the intention of play, whereas the game's outside is assessed in terms of functionality. This calls for a closer analysis of the relation between play, pedagogy and power communication in the different games and for a discussion of the inherent problem in the games of explicitly stating their functional intention. It is characteristic for almost all the games that they seek to conceal the organizer and creator of the games. What is the logic behind this? Why is this a persistent trend? We will address these questions in the next chapter.

5
The Coupling of Play, Power and Pedagogy

Introduction

The question in this chapter is: In what ways are play, power and pedagogy coupled in creation games? The previous chapter necessitates an enquiry into the relation between play and power. Does power define play or is it the other way around so that power is now played into existence? But it also seems necessary to include the logic of pedagogy in the analysis because, contrary to the training games of the 1960s where play became pedagogized, the new creation games seem to empty pedagogy of all content so that it is merely a question of learning, and play is perceived as learning per definition. Furthermore, the pedagogical observations of play as learning and creating seem to support the new power perspective on play. Therefore, I will not only discuss the relation between the logic of play and power but also try to capture the hegemonic form, which causes play, power and pedagogy together to establish a new regime.

I distinguish between three fundamentally different forms of communication: play, power and pedagogy. I discuss the way in which the different semantics of play establish different combinations of these forms of communication and the possible effects of these.

I begin by analysing the forms of power and pedagogy as two distinctive forms of communication in addition to the form of play, which I have already analysed in Chapter 3. Then I go on to analyse the couplings between play, pedagogy and power. Here, I draw on the entire semantic history as presented in Chapter 2 and not only the topical semantics about social creation games. Thus, I do not only

137

discuss topical possibilities for couplings in relation to creation games and political games but also explore the way in which these possibilities for couplings have changed over time, including how the new coupling affects the forms of both pedagogy and power.

In conclusion, I discuss power as the outside of play. I conclude that the current conditions of power force it to try to make itself invisible. Power has to suspend itself in order to be able to re-emerge in a new functional form. And play is precisely the means to achieve this.

1. Power as form

Luhmann has carried out extensive analyses of power as a form of communication (Luhmann 1979). He argues that the modern form of power has the character of a communicative code that divides the world into those who steer and those are steered, where it is of course better to steer than to be steered. Or in more general terms: The code of power divides the world into power-superiority (+) and power-inferiority (−) where power-superiority represents power's positive and motivating value (how to achieve power and exercise power) and where power-inferiority represents the reflective value of power (what do they want with me and how did I end up in the inferior position? But also: what do I want with power?). When communicating through power as form, one can only link up on one of the two sides. Power is not power-superiority or power-inferiority but precisely the relation between them. Power is the unity of power-superiority and power-inferiority.

Power is often confused with coercion, but power-superiority is not the same as coercion and cannot be obtained through coercion. By contrast, power as power presupposes precisely the absence of coercion. There can be no relation between power-superiority and power-inferiority without the exclusion of coercion.

There are several concomitant points here. The first one is that modern power consists in the ability for the power-superior to shift complexity onto the power-inferior. This is fundamentally different than coercion as it operates, for example, in a slave-master relationship, where coercion consists in the master forcing the slave to perform a specific act. The coercion of the slave-master relationship presupposes, as analysed in the Roman *The Life of Aesop* (Æsopromanen 2003) from the fifth century BC, a very physically present, precise, and direct action against the one who is forced to act. By contrast, the advantage of modern power is that it is able to shift complexity from the power-superior onto the power-inferior, who have to carry and handle this complexity in a continued interpretation of the intentions of the power-superior.

In modern management, for example, power may consist in a manager asking an employee to deliver a concept for future employee performance reviews. That is the only instruction provided by the manager. The manager might not even define a general objective. Therefore, the employee spends a great deal of time trying to figure out what the manager's intention is. What could she have meant? In this way, the employee manages himself through a continued interpretation of the manager's possible intentions. More than likely, the manager didn't have clear intentions. Management intentions come into existence through working with the concept in the power-inferior's interpretation of the intentions of the power-superior. These can then later be confirmed or rejected in the manager's reception of the concept (it is really good or it does not work!). Therefore, the power-superior does not need to handle a particularly large share of the factual complexity associated with employee performance reviews but is able to send this complexity down through the organizational hierarchy together with a sense of uncertainty with respect to the intentions of the power-superior. As soon as the inferior reaches a position where pressure may be put on the manager to express her wishes, the manager's power is reduced.

The precondition for such complexity transfer is the absence of coercion. When coercion is used, the inferior is left with neither choice of action nor choice of interpretation of the intentions of the power-superior. Luhmann expresses it this way: 'Power arises under condition of *double contingency* on both sides of the relation. This means that for *the person who has power* as well as for *the person who is subordinate to it* the relation must be so defined that both could act otherwise. Thus in this sense: double double contingency' (Luhmann 1990: 156). Stated in more simple terms this means that power presupposes the freedom of the power-inferior. If the power-inferior is not free, he is not able to steer himself in the interpretation of the intentions of the power-superior. Modern power is simply based on self-steering and the freedom of the subject: 'Power increases with freedom on *both* sides' (Luhmann 1979: 113). Here, Luhmann is in complete agreement with Michel Foucault when, for example, Foucault says: 'One must observe also that there cannot be relations of power unless the subject is free. If one or the other were completely at the disposition of the other and became his thing, an object on which he can exercise an infinite an unlimited violence, there would not be relations of power. In order to exercise a relation of power, there must be on both sides at least a certain form of liberty' (Foucault 1988: 12).

Power is exercised when the power-inferior feels unsure about the power-superior and steers himself from the perspective of the possible intentions of the power-superior. Thus, power presupposes the freedom of the power-inferior. Power means to steer on the basis of the freedom of others. The greater the capacity for self-steering in the power-inferior, the greater the overall potential for power. Coercion is the constitutive outside of power. Coercion means complete power in its elimination of freedom as such. Modern power is non-coercion. Coercion has to always be present as an alternative to power in the form of sanctions, but as soon as the power-superior employs sanctions, the complexity falls back onto the power-superior who has to suddenly admit her intentions. Or as Luhmann puts it: 'Power, therefore, comes to an end if the exercise of this possibility can be forced. The exercise of physical violence is not an application of power but an expression of its failure – or, at best, a presentation of considered possibility of being able to apply sanctions repeatedly' (Luhmann 1990: 158).

I have tried to formalize and sum up the form of power in the illustration shown in Figure 5.1.

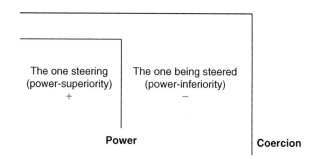

Figure 5.1   The form of power

Figure 5.1 illustrates that power is the unity of power-superiority and power-inferiority and that coercion represents the constitutive outside of power. Coercion is necessary as non-realizable possibility. Without the possibility for coercion as a negative sanction it would not be possible to maintain the operative difference between power-inferiority and power-superiority. But at the same time, any crossing of the difference from the side of power to the side of coercion would cancel out the difference between power-superiority and power-inferiority. In other words, coercion is a necessary impossibility for the constitution of communicative power relations.

2. Pedagogy as form

Luhmann analyses pedagogy as a form of communication in several writings and he has revised it several times. Here, I will primarily focus on his early form analysis of pedagogy, which I perceive as much more conceptually tight than the later analyses. Like the form of power, the form of pedagogy has the character of a communicative code that divides the world into a positive motivational value and a negative reflective value. This distinction is better/worse in terms of learning.

Pedagogical communication forms a specific general symbolic medium of communication, that is, 'the child' (Luhmann 1993b). A special history pertains to the emergence of the distinction between child and adult. There has not always been such a distinction. Children were at one point regarded simply as small adults (Ariés 1973). The modern notion of the relation child/adult was formed in the 1700s and disbands the idea that the child becomes what it is born to become. This notion is replaced by the notion that the child can be formed. What the child becomes is now seen as dependent on the environment that forms the child. This leads to the development of the now classic discussion about nature or nurture, which is fundamentally a discussion about the plasticity of the child: how great is the effect of education and upbringing on the fate and formation of the individual child? The possibility of observing the child as mouldable creates the conditions for pedagogical communication in which one does not actually talk *with* the child, but where the 'child' lets itself be represented as the symbol of a learning effort. The child becomes a symbol that one communicates by means of. The child is the *medium* to be *moulded* in pedagogical communication.

What the child is to be moulded into depends on the pedagogical programme. The moulding may pertain to compliance, morality, creativity, subject knowledge or something entirely different. The fact that the child as a medium is a *general* symbolic medium of communication means that there are no restrictions for the kinds of knowledge that can be imprinted into the medium. In principle, the child can be moulded into anything, into a tyrant, an artist, an environmentalist, etc. That the medium is *symbolic* means that the child is the symbolic and recognizable expression of the medium, that is, that which we might communicate about. However, the symbol is variable and can be replaced by, for example, student, pupil, or course participant (and does not therefore depend on biological age). Regardless of the symbol, the distinction follows: child/adult ≈ mouldable/finished.

The binary *code* that the child as medium carries with it is better/worse in terms of learning (Luhmann 1989: 100–106). In pedagogical communication, everything is observed from that perspective. Everything is observed with a view to perfection. Thus, it is *a corrective code* where one is able to link up either to the code's positive preference value, e.g. by considering ways in which for the student/pupil/course participant to become better at this or that, or link up to the code's reflective side in thoughts on why things are not working out considering that we have embraced the most current pedagogical methods. Moreover, the code is of course also used in continual evaluations and testing of the child's competencies: passed/failed, strong/weak sides, etc. In any case pedagogical communication becomes a question of correcting with a view to perfection.

When communicating pedagogically, the objective is to mould a subject who is treated like a child, that is, as something that can be moulded. Whether this subject is in fact a child, a student, an apprentice, or an employee involved in 'lifelong learning', the moulding is actually beyond the reach of the pedagogical communication. Pedagogical communication is able to observe what the student says and does, but pedagogy is unable to observe what the student thinks about what takes place in the teaching situation. From the perspective of the communication, the student's consciousness represents a 'black box'. Pedagogical communication can link up to another pedagogical communication but is unable to link up to thought operations in conscious systems and therefore cannot control them. Pedagogical communication can teach and revise its teaching on the basis of observation, but ultimately it is unable to teach pupils, students, or employees anything because their learning consists in what they choose to do with what they are being taught. Therefore, pedagogical communication draws yet another distinction between pedagogy and teaching on one side and socialization on the other. Socialization is observed in pedagogy as the child's 'natural' education and adaptation within society. The shaping of socialization is what pedagogical communication is fundamentally about. Socialization that is not shaped by pedagogy is perceived as high-risk. The children are not shaped, not shaped enough, or shaped inappropriately. It is crucial to pedagogy, therefore, to give the socialization a specific direction, but at the same time socialization can never be more than the constitutive outside of pedagogy. Pedagogy desires socialization but has to limit itself to making a distinction between better or worse in terms of learning. Figure 5.2 shows how the form of pedagogy can be illustrated.

Of course, pedagogy may reflect upon the notion of socialization and try in various ways to appropriate it. Modern pedagogy performs a re-entry of the code of pedagogy into itself and develops doctrines for learning to learn in the same way that it begins to focus on social and personal preconditions for learning. This leads to the development of concepts about social and personal competencies and about the many different aspects of intelligence, such as for example Howard Gardner's theory about multiple intelligences (Gardner 1997). However, socialization still remains the untouchable outside of pedagogy.

From the perspective of pedagogy, play becomes a functional aspect of socialization. Children socialize themselves through play, and in pedagogical theories play represents, therefore, a kind of coupling

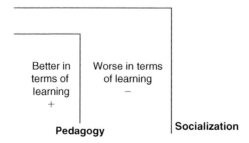

Figure 5.2   The form of pedagogy

between biology and sociality. Play represents a biological drive in the child, which forces the child into a process of socialization. Although socialization is the constitutive outside of pedagogy, pedagogy believes itself to be able to observe socialization mechanisms in order to change them into pedagogical technologies. The observation that children become socialized through play can be used pedagogically to improve teaching by incorporating elements of play into it. And with this, we are already moving in the direction of the coupling analysis.

3. Couplings: playing oneself into power

I am working with three communication forms shown in Figure 5.3: play, power, and pedagogy.

My claim is that the three play semantics we have looked at in a historical perspective (competitive games, training games and creation games) indicate in radically different ways the coupling of the communication forms of power, play and pedagogy. I do not claim that the semantics determine the couplings. It is important to remember that semantics are reservoirs of concepts available to communication, which communication is therefore able to use. Semantics is simply suggestions for expectation structures. Semantics does not operate. Only communication operates and communication has a life of its own. A game also represents a semantic structure. Playing Monopoly does not prescribe the way in which the communication takes shape. Rules can be circumvented, and if there are children playing the game, they might from time to time get away with something or the grownups might let them move their pieces a little further than prescribed

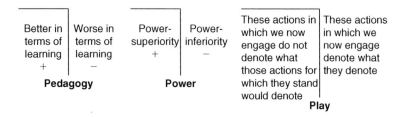

Figure 5.3   Three forms

by the role of the dice so that they will not end up in jail or something else. Or the children might open the Monopoly box but only end up playing with the monopoly money. They might end up playing store instead. A game is a suggested structure. How and whether they come to structure a given situation is determined solely by communication.

As I have outlined in Chapter 3, a coupling is not something that exists between systems. A system can only be coupled to another system by performing this coupling internally by making itself sensitive to the communication of other systems. Couplings, therefore, are always systems-internal elements, and when studying couplings, one studies the conditions for systems' ability to be interrupted by each other.

I am going to work with a distinction between parasitary coupling, loose coupling, fixed coupling and hegemonic coupling.

A *parasitary coupling* is in fact not even a coupling. Instead, I will discuss how a system becomes a parasite on another system – when system A unambiguously links up to system B's motivational side and only perceives B of instrumental benefit for A. This becomes apparent if system A does not relate to the reflections of system B. A observes B as a benefit without independent functionality. A classic example of a parasitary communication could be when a political party wraps its position in a political debate in scientific arguments without opening up for possible errors in the applied knowledge. The parasitary aspect in this example is that truth is not observed as a value in itself but only as a benefit in relation to a political standpoint.

Loose coupling occurs in a system when it observes the operations of another system without responding with any commitment to structure. System A has built up conditions letting itself be interrupted by system B, but it has not developed any stable expectations with respect to a precise response to the irritation. Loose couplings may of course be present in several systems at once, which results in a situation where several systems observe each other and let themselves be interrupted by each other and thus create order up against each other's interruptions without causing the interruptions to take place routinely or redundantly. One example could be the issuing of fines in response to a violation of environmental regulation. The law observes the fines as a behaviour prescription. The fine indicates that an illegal action has taken place and that certain behaviour should be prescribed. However, in economic communication, the fines are productively misread as price fixing in relation to a specific activity. As a loose coupling, however, it has not been structurally defined how the economic systems should respond to fines, only whether the fines should be paid, be budgeted or avoided.

Fixed coupling occurs in a system when it observes the operations of another system and responds with structural commitment. This might take place in several systems at the same time. In a fixed coupling the mutual interruptions between the systems of communication are mediated by a third form, which incorporates redundancy and routine into the coupling. One example could be a contract, which does not only couple law and economy in individual situations but creates redundancy in the coupling throughout the contract period. A contract is not located in between the systems. A contract consists of mutual obligations, but these obligations are not perceived in the same way by the involved systems. In order for a contract to function as fixed coupling it has to be recognizable as contract by several different systems simultaneously. The systems even have to be able to recognize the contract in each other's communications, but at the same time each communication has to remain sufficiently free to provide the contract with its systems-internal meaning. In other words, a contract only exists in the afterlife which it achieves in the continued communications about the contract in the economic system and the legal system respectively. Economy communicates about the contract as an exchange whereas the law communicates about the contract as a promise, and in the redundant coupling, furthermore, the law can communicate about the economy's communication about the contract in a productive misreading of the exchange, perceived as the exchange of promises. And in the same way, economy can communicate about legal communication about the contract perceives as transaction costs (Andersen 2008a).

Hegemonic coupling exists when a form of communication couples itself together with other forms and subsumes these under its own form. Thus, hegemonic coupling is a fixed coupling where one of the mutual forms systematically produces occasions for coupling. A hegemonic coupling, therefore, is one that parasites on the couplings of other systems. Thus, the hegemonic system also produces the fixed couplings of the other systems. The four different types of coupling are shown schematically in Figure 5.4.

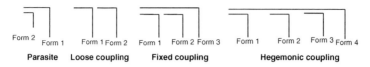

Figure 5.4 Couplings

Competition games: power parasites on the code of play

The competition games from the first phase primarily involve play on the unambiguous terms of power. When organizing competitions for salespeople or price committees for specific professions, this does not entail any form of 'free play'. Play is observed through the code of power as a way to symbolize certain values, e.g. the value of high sales numbers, the value of competition or the value of professional marketing campaigns. But the games do not entail playing with values. Inherent in play as a form is 'going meta', that is, asking: Is this play? However, from the perspective of power communication about competition games this 'going meta' is observed as dysfunctionality. There are repeated discussions of the risks of play when it takes on a life of its own. When salespeople take the competitions too seriously, the competition games are no longer seen as morale building but instead as detrimental. When employees involve themselves and really engage in the effort to win, then the competitive mentality is seen as detrimental. The measure of whether competition games are seen as functional or dysfunctional in this phase is always located outside the games in the sphere of power. From the perspective of power, competition games have to be controlled. Once the games take on a life of their own, power sees an uncontrollability that has to be overcome. In other words, play is not recognized for its own functionality. Play has to empower but is not supposed to play with power. We can speak, therefore, of a coupling of power and play in which power parasites on play as form. Play is only brought into play as a controlled artefact. An illustration of this is shown in Figure 5.5.

Training games: pedagogy parasites on the code of play

The training games from the 1950s suggest a rather different coupling. At the same time, it indicates a certain level of continuity because power still parasites on play by observing it as object and

Figure 5.5   Power parasites on play

as symbolization technique. However, the training games also install a different perspective: that of pedagogy. So in addition to being subordinated to power as form, play now also becomes subordinated to pedagogy as form. Play is pedagogized! Playing always entails a learning related objective, and the objectives are not only general but also often very specific. The games are always about training and achieving competencies in relation to a particular decision maker role.

The reason for playing is to imbue learning with particular attractive qualities. Play is observed from the perspective of pedagogy. That is why the games do not refer to play in positive terms, but instead to games. The games should be fun and exciting, but they should not take on the qualities of play. If playing is too much fun and draws attention away from the learning objective, then playing is considered dysfunctional. That is why there are discussions about making certain games more boring. The games in themselves should not be too exciting. Games are able to create engagement and that is considered a good thing in the eyes of pedagogy. However, a game also has the ability to over-engage if the game takes over and becomes an objective in and of itself. That is pedagogically dysfunctional. Clearly, therefore, these games suggest that pedagogy as form parasites on play as form without granting play its own life and functionality.

However, the training games also invoke a different coupling question with respect to pedagogy and power. This I will define as a loose coupling in which pedagogy and power can unfold themselves as independent forms of communication in a productive reading of each other's communication. That happens in relation to the notion of role. From the perspective of power, communication roles, particularly decision maker roles, represent a way to link specific persons

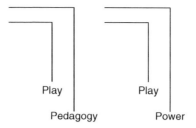

Play   Play
Pedagogy   Power

Figure 5.6   Pedagogy parasites on play, and power and pedagogy are loosely coupled

to specific responsibilities and distribute responsibility in the organization. Roles are a way to establish relations of superiority and subordination. From the perspective of pedagogy, on the other hand, roles can be observed as professions, which require the acquisition of specific competencies. Roles have to be learned. Thus, roles function as programmes for pedagogical communication. In power communication, pedagogy can be perceived as disciplining, that is, as a service in relation to ensuring the best possible subordination of the person in relation to the role. Pedagogy in turn can read power communication as specifications of the role and its preconditions. Play's subordination to pedagogy and pedagogy's loose coupling to power can be illustrated together as in Figure 5.6.

The figure illustrates pedagogy and power as parallel forms that can irritate each other in a productive way because it is continually kept unclear in the communication whether communication is about power or pedagogy. The figure shows play as both parasitarily subordinated to the form of pedagogy and parasitarily subordinated to the form of power. However, play is parasiting in two different ways. In pedagogy, play works as an attractor. From the perspective of power, however, play represents a symbolization form. Pedagogy flirts with the inside of play, its capacity to produce dedication and engagement, but pedagogy does not accept the form of play as such, including play's doubling of the world in a play reality and real reality privileging the play side of the distinction.

Social creation games: play is set free
In social creation games, couplings are radically different because they recognize play's independent value and functionality. Even the word

'play' has here become positively defined in the same way that the games often employ child symbolism. The distinction between play and seriousness is now defined from the perspective of play so that the games play with seriousness. Play starts to be judged on its own premises. However, this does not mean that play is no longer also observed from the perspective of power and pedagogy. We will return to this below. But the creation games are also discussed from the perspective of play, that is, on the basis of the question 'Is this play?', 'Is this for fun?' etc. Therefore, dysfunctionality can now be viewed in the language of play. To Ken Jones, a game is dysfunctional, and even pathological, if the participants are led to believe that something is a game and it turns out not to be judged as such (Jones 1994). If an activity is at once defined as play and non-play, the game may seem like a violation to the participants. Play can turn pathological if an act in one instance does not denote that which the act would otherwise denote and in the next instance denotes precisely that which the act denotes. An example could be a therapeutic game in which participants play with personal future scenarios and present different potential scenarios in the spirit of the game only to then be held to their words and kept responsible for the realization of these scenarios.

In the creation games, one plays with seriousness, and for the most part the games also suggest that one may play with the boundaries of the game. They encourage meta-play. The creation games can play with themselves as play; the games are often designed in a way so that they evolve as they are played and transform into something other than they were imagined to be. Although there is also a serious intent behind the initiation of creation games, there is usually room for playing with this seriousness and an opportunity to transform the serious reason for playing into a seriousness defined and mediated by the game itself. The objectives of the creation games are far from as strictly formulated as in the training games. The objectives are far more general and geared exclusively toward reflection and therefore more open to reinterpretation through the process of the game, and to the extent that the organizations and their elements make up the seriousness of the game these are not perceived as being outside the game. Creation games imply playing with the organization, its strategies, distribution of roles, mission, etc. And even more than that, creation games also make it possible in different ways to play with communication forms outside play such as pedagogy and power. In creation games, play parasites on the forms of power and pedagogy. From the perspective of play, as it is, communication, which denotes that which it denotes, is a source of play. From the perspective of play, denotations represent both the boundary of play as well as the material for play. We could say that play couples itself to the communication of power and pedagogy from within by playing with their denotations. When playing 'Possible predictions', play does not only let itself be interrupted by pedagogical communication, it even plays with pedagogy as form and with the notion of defining personal goals for learning. And 'Slave for a day' or 'Shared responsibility' play with relations of subordination and superiority. These games play with power. From the perspective of pedagogy, this is seen as experimental learning and creativity. And from the perspective of power communication, it is seen as empowerment.

In addition, play is loosely coupled to pedagogy in creation games. As already mentioned, play can link up to pedagogical communication by playing with it. Pedagogy may also link to creation games, but the implied coupling is entirely different from the one in the training games. In the training games, a pedagogy parasite on play, and play was considered primarily to have value as attractor and as a way to create excitement. In the creation games, however, play is observable from the perspective of pedagogy in a different way because there has been a slight change in the form of pedagogy in relation to the creation games. It is a pedagogical form of communication that has tied itself into a knot so to speak.

The pedagogical perspective on the creation games does not see these games as a pedagogical technique designed to learn specific competencies in relation to a professional role. The question is much more about learning to learn with a focus on personal and social development. From the perspective of pedagogy, these games are not about learning a given skill or competence, but about seeing oneself as competent and adopting a pedagogical view of oneself and of one's perspectives on the world. When observed pedagogically, creation games are about transforming the relation between pedagogy as form (the code) and the medium of pedagogy (the child) into an internal self-relation in the participants. The participants are invited to divide themselves into form and medium. They have to present themselves as both strategists of self-development and as competence objectives in themselves. The goal is to define the individual as the moulder of himself as medium: to become educator and child at the same time! In order to achieve this, the self-relation has to be codified pedagogically so that it entails the reflection upon oneself as object for learning within the code better/worse in terms of learning. Being competent means to develop personal competences, thus signifying the ability to see oneself as unfinished. Therefore, the central competence no longer resides in the relation between the individual and an external object that has to be mastered but in the individual's self-relation and mastery with respect to that relation. Pedagogical revision, therefore, comes to equal the revision of one's self-relation! One has to view one's self and personality as something incomplete that has to be continually developed. This at some point means seeing oneself as a child (Andersen 2004a, 2005, 2007b). The code of pedagogy is re-entered into itself and can be diagrammatically represented as shown in Figure 5.7.

Observed from the perspective of the folded-in form, play is not just something that makes learning exciting. The nature of play is now seen as a form of learning. Play is considered as self-socialization. In relation to the goal of teaching the participants to learn in such a way that they become able to view themselves pedagogically, social games are viewed as a fundamentally positive thing. Play creates self-esteem. Play provides new perspectives on oneself, on others and on relationships. Play opens up, throws new light, and promotes physical reflexivity. Play is vitality and creativity in one. Play in itself represents all these things. These positive aspects can then be further strengthened if the games are supervised in a consciously pedagogical way. We could say that with creation games, pedagogy sets play free from the

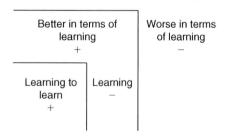

Figure 5.7   The form of pedagogy folded back on to itself

perspective that play is always learning, and at the same time pedagogy defines itself as process supervisor. And this happens precisely
through the form of play where someone does not play firefighter but
plays with the notion of playing firefighter. In other words, creativity
has moved upward and outward. Supervision becomes a question of
playing with the notion of play.

Learning objectives in social creation games have become general,
empty and self-referential. It might for example be defined as a learning objective to develop (but not in which direction), to innovate
(but not what), to change perspective (but not which perspectives),
to engage in dialogue and cooperation (but not about what) and to
articulate emotions and relations (but not which words to use). The
more specific learning objectives are to be played into existence. One
does not need to learn specific things, but one has to learn to be
learning. One might even say that pedagogy has been emptied out
and functions merely as facilitator and supervisor of play.

How does this effect power/play? Power communication in creation
games provides others with the possibility for productively observing
play based on the notion that the form of power, like the form of pedagogy, has tied itself into a knot. The creation games repeatedly reflect
upon empowerment. From the perspective of power, creation games
are about stimulating and steering the power-inferior's way of creating himself as self-steered. Families must be made capable of steering
themselves from a health perspective. Third-world children must be
given self-esteem, knowledge and experiences about their ability to
change their lives through responsible action, particularly communal
action. Employees must learn to see themselves in the future and take
action in relation to their development. Empowerment implies, therefore, a re-entry of the code of power steering (power-superior)/steered
(power-inferior) on the side of steering. It implies a doubling of power,
where the difference between steering and steered is copied and is
re-entered into itself in such a way so that the object of steering
becomes the creation of self-steering in the steered. The form of
power becomes the power over the power-inferior's power-relation
to himself. Barbara Cruikshank has provided a rich description of
the empowerment logic in her book about the will to empowerment,
which is a critical and cynical study of empowerment in the United
States, both in liberal women's movements and among conservative
groups fighting poverty. She argues that the empowerment figure

focuses on the lack of self-esteem and on the way in which power is exercised by the power-inferior against themselves. The background for this, she argues, is the establishment of a specific logic or perspective that divides the world into the empowered and the powerless. The empowered can only be fabricated on the basis of powerlessness (Cruikshank 1999: 71). In order to empower the power-inferior, these have to be observed as powerless without independent will. The doubling of power into power and empowerment is illustrated in Figure 5.8.

Whereas pedagogy's drive for socialization results in the pedagogization of self-relation and the social, the drive of power for complete hegemony (coercion) results in empowerment, that is, in the attempt to seize control of the power-inferior's self-creation as an empowered subordinate. Power communication is basically a form of communication in which actions act in response to actions. However, from an empowerment perspective the power-inferior is considered to be unable to act on the actions of the power-superior. Empowerment, therefore, is about creating and qualifying the power-inferior as capable of action.

Here we see another parallel to pedagogy's folding back on to itself; in the same way that pedagogy in its doubled form is emptied out so that it is no longer a question of learning *something* but of *being* learning, one may argue that empowerment is not a question of having the power to do something but simply of being empowered. That means that power, too, is emptied out and becomes self-referential when it assumes the form of empowerment.

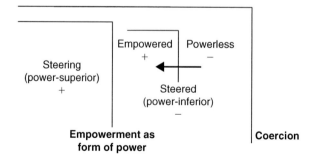

Figure 5.8   Empowerment

Empowerment is power communication that observes itself as liberating. Empowerment is power communication that renders itself invisible as power by concealing the difference between steering/steered behind the objective of empowerment. In all modern exercise of power, freedom is a precondition of effective power communication because power, as we have argued above, operates through the power-inferior's administration of own freedom in the interpretation of the power-superior's possible intentions. Moreover, the empowerment logic seeks to seize control of the very creation of freedom, the individual's creation of himself as free, and thus the independently acting actor. The empowerment logic seeks to regulate the language of freedom and existence.

In order to be able to do this effectively, power communication cannot be visibly present. It has to communicate through stand-in forms. From the perspective of empowerment, play represents such a form, which simultaneously allows power to become invisible and to direct itself towards power as self-creation.

Empowerment focuses on the self-creation of the power-inferior. The headlines are self-esteem, self-development, self-satisfaction, self-management, etc. In this perspective, play is productive power. Play is seen precisely as vital, positive and creative. Since play even signals the absence of power because what we say in the game does not mean what it usually means, play contributes to the invisibility of power. One cannot play on cue, says Huizinga but creation games say, 'I think you should play' (Huizinga 1971).

In creation games, empowerment is not only directed at the individual whether in the capacity of citizen or employee. Empowerment is also directed at collectives such as the team, a work community, a partnership, a parent group, a partner or a village community. Playing visions and strategies into existence is a way to empower collectives. With empowerment also meaning self-empowerment in relation to the position of the power-superior, which can now be directed towards freedom, which otherwise would be out of reach in the exclusion of coercion, perceived as the outside of power.

Similarly, a pedagogy that is folded back on itself and implies a self-childification of the individual who has to view herself with pedagogical development eyes may easily be observed as an empowerment technology. Pedagogy is observed in the eyes of empowerment as a contribution to the creation of empowered actors.

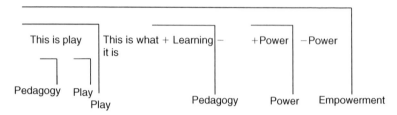

Figure 5.9   Empowerment couples pedagogy, play, and power

We may sum this up by saying that the empowerment perspective recognizes the independent functionality of play and pedagogy respectively, but at the same time, it is through the form of empowerment that play, pedagogy, and power are linked together and coupled in a productive way. Thus, empowerment becomes the hegemonic form that couples the other forms in mutually productive interruptions. Figure 5.9 shows an illustration of this.

4. Conclusion: the invisibility and self-suspension of power

The hegemonic coupling form produces, however, certain paradoxes associated with the necessary invisibility of empowerment. As I have already stated, empowerment is power communication that renders itself invisible as power by hiding the difference steering/steered behind the intention to empower.

This rendering invisible, however, pertains to two additional issues. One issue relates to the logic of play. When creation games are actualized as the strategy for empowerment, it leads to another problem of invisibility. Power has to be rendered invisible in relation to the communication of pedagogy and, in particular, in relation to the communication of play. As Huizinga points out, it is difficult to play on cue (Huizinga 1971). However, when private companies and political authorities organize social creation games, this is precisely what is at stake. Power is the god of play but cannot show itself.

The other issue is that the object, which the creation games seek to seize power of, resides beyond the reach of power. Creation games have directed themselves at (1) objects that did not recognize themselves as power-inferior in relation to the game organizer, (2) objects that were unsuited as power-inferior, or (3) objects, preferred by the game organizer, who were self-managing and self-steering and therefore should not recognize the power-superior as superior since this would fundamentally question the capacity for self-management. Games such as 'Health at play' and 'The game of responsibility' from the municipality of Aarhus belong to the first category. In these games, parents do not usually recognize themselves as subordinate in relation to the school except for a few rather specific obligations such as making sure that their children get to school. But the parents do not fundamentally see the family as subordinate in relation to the school. In 'Health at play', the school also does not recognize itself as subordinate in relation to the National Board of Health and in 'Values at stake', the volunteers do not perceive of themselves as employees subordinated to a manager in their voluntary organization. In fact, they more often perceive the voluntary organization as theirs. The second category of creation games include the many games within the therapeutic strategy directed at employees and citizens who are considered to have low self-esteem, poor will-power, and lack the will to adapt. These people also need to be empowered in order to qualify themselves for a relation of subordination and superiority. *Right to Play* also belongs to this category. It plays with third-world children who are not considered qualified in their role as power-inferiors, but who also do not see themselves as power-inferior. And finally, to the third category of games belong team building games and change management games, e.g. 'Team discovery' and 'Shaping the future' in which employees, project groups, partners and others who could be identified as power-inferior and who would recognize themselves in this identification, but who are not identified as such because the aim of the game is self-management and self-creation of subsystems capable of defining own strategies, vision, means and ends.

In all three cases, the power-superior is unable to communicate her position without simultaneously undermining it. The school cannot, whether in soft or hard terms, dictate a healthy life for the family. The school can also not demand that parents organize camping trips, outings, and other get-togethers in order to ensure the best school environment. The school cannot instruct parents to play educational role models who read books, do not smoke or drink, but take long walks and eat lots of fruit. If the school has any power ambition in this respect, it has to veil it so it is not visible to the parents.

Private companies that wish to increase their flexibility and adaptability through cross-disciplinary teams also have to withhold communication of specific intentions in order to actually build teams that take responsibility for and manage themselves. Here, it becomes necessary to relinquish the power one actually holds. Power suspends itself in order to become possible in a new way (Philippopulos-Mihalopoulos 2003). Again, power has to be rendered invisible in order not to appear dysfunctional. It is a question of the powerlessness of the position of power-superiority. In many instances, there is simply no position from which power can be held.

Without a position from which to hold power, the central effort becomes to create conditions for subordination and superiority. It is precisely these conditions that the creation games play with which is precisely the core of playing oneself into power. Therefore, from a power perspective, which in this case coincides with a perspective of powerlessness, creation games are about establishing every condition for making power communication possible. Which means the empowerment of the power-inferior, self-empowerment of the power-superior, and the intentionality of power in the form of strategies, visions, etc.; that is, in both positions and expectations. At the same time, however, this installs the vulnerability of power because 'we are only playing!'

Conclusion: Power at Play

In my analysis I have shown the way in which, first of all, a new organizational language has emerged, which articulates play as an important element in modern organization and management. This language did not develop overnight. It has evolved gradually since the mid-1800s but has also undergone significant shifts. From the 1860s on we can observe the development of semantics in the context of competition games in organizations. This was the beginning of company sports. There are no monetary competitions between salespeople and buyers, but experimentation with competitions in the workplaces. This language articulates play as a way for organizations to symbolize and discipline competition as a phenomenon. From 1950 until 1980 a language about training and simulation games in organizations developed. This language makes a distinction between play and games, where play is not acceptable but where games can be tied to organizational objectives. Games are seen as a way for organizations to professionalize their employees' training for management roles. Finally a language that developed in the 1980s, about play as an organizational power of self-organization, a kind of power of spontaneity, continues today. Play is seen as the core of the organization's creation of itself as an organization and of the employees' self-creation, both as people and employees. This last phase reflects on the organization's social dimension, temporal dimension, as well as factual dimension in social creation games. Reality is not something that is represented in play. Play is itself a reality in which the organizational reality is played into existence. The creation games imply that organizational elements are played into existence, from visions and strategies via internal and external partnerships to teams for employee attitudes, cooperation and winner mentality. Moreover, many different strategies for organizational games seem to crystallize, including a therapeutic strategy, a teambuilding strategy and a strategy about fun in the workplace and the right attitude.

Next, I analysed play and decisions as two distinct forms of communication. I analysed the communication form of decision as the unity of fixed social contingency and open social contingency. Decision communication responds to social expectations by fixing them, but at the same time each fixing of social expectations opens up for the possibility that a different decision could have been made. Play is an entirely different communication form that doubles the world into a play world and a real world. Play is sociality, which at the same time defines sociality as its outside, which means that play continually draws attention to the contingency of the social. There is a constant meta-communication within play that says 'this is play'. Outside play, actions denote that which they denote. In play, on the other hand, actions denote other actions without denoting that which these actions would otherwise denote.

I then analysed the strange coupling that happens in social creation games between decision as a form of communication and play as a form of communication. Decisions themselves cannot play. Only play can play. All decisions can do is to respond to something and thereby set social expectations. To the extent that creation games actually result in play, e.g. with the organization's strategy, that play does not in fact take place within the organization since play establishes its own universe. Through games, therefore, the organization is able to become free from itself. The autopoiesis of play represents the organization's chance to circumvent itself as a restriction and barrier for its own adaptability. Creation games make possible a displacement of the organization's production of premises in the direction of differentiated play interaction. But play and decision stabilizes communication in very different ways. Decisions bind energy by fixing expectations whereas play becomes binding through the energy produced by the game. The result of this can be the organization at play, which on one hand is made up of a decided organization and on the other hand a multiplicity of games each with an imaginary universe of their own. The organization at play allows for the formation of a multiplicity of fluctuating subsystems, playing forth various suggestions for organizational elements that can be maintained as suggestions through continued play or be received and organized as decided decision premises. Play, therefore, is a form of integration that seems to double the organization into a formal organization and a virtual multiplicity, an organization that can oscillate endlessly between the virtual and the formal binding, between non-commitment and commitment. And even more radical: Play emerges as a *generalized* perspective on the organization, a general gaze which can enlighten all aspect of the organization in any moment turning decisions premises into virtuality! The organization becomes self-deconstructive increasing it capacity for always being something other than what it is, perhaps even to be something other than an organization. It is a form of organization that signs away its own unambiguous unity and obtains a different multiple unity, which becomes possible precisely because it is just something we are playing; that is, because the sub-systems are the games and their results virtual. They play organization but do not constitute one.

In Chapter four I analysed a number of political games. Above all, what was interesting about these games was that they suggested that boundaries had to be played into existence. The first two games were intended for use in voluntary organizations. In slightly different ways, these games invite volunteers to establish and reflect upon boundaries for volunteer work. The game 'Values at play' even offers different reflexive layers in which the dilemmas of volunteer work become dependent on specific perspectives. The dilemmas become polycontextual and come to depend on whether they are articulated in the voice of morality, law, spirituality, love or friendship. Generally, however, the organization has withdrawn from its role as the creator of decision premises. The volunteers are invited to take on a personal commitment with respect to the boundaries and positions they play into existence in the game. Whether or not one chooses to play is voluntary, but playing the game means a commitment. And that instils a paradox for both volunteers and their organization: should volunteer games be taken seriously as a commitment or are they precisely just games and play that do not represent a commitment on the part of both organization and volunteer? Next, I analysed two games from the Danish public school system. Like a Trojan horse, the first game, 'Short and sweet in the family', is ordained by the school but played by the family in their home. I showed how the game encourages the articulation of the family's creation of itself, its mutual relations, and its boundaries. The second game, 'The game of responsibility', is played in a school setting at parent meetings. It is a dialogue game through which parents exchange opinions about the placement of responsibility between school and home. The game pretends to be about making different expectations visible with respect to school and home and the cooperation between them, but it concludes by suddenly reifying its discussions as decision. Play suddenly becomes decision. What the parents play into existence during the course of the game, is suddenly perceived by the teachers at the end of the game as a decision, which is then written down and made applicable for that specific class. Next, I described a game from the International NGO *Right to Play*. The game is basically about inviting children to play forth resourceful communities, communities that are both powerful and empowering for the individual. The intention is to support play that can play civil society into existence both on a local and global level and thereby establish a community and collective responsibility concerning issues of peacekeeping and health development. The boundary put at play is the one between individual and community. Finally, I analysed the game 'Health at play', produced for the National Board of Health and the Ministry for Food, Agriculture and Fisheries but intended for use at parent events in Danish public schools. The game aims to make families, students, and school look at themselves from a health perspective and to establish agreements about the division of responsibility in relation to children's health. The game is designed in a way so that it presents itself as play, but it results in a collective agreement about specific health responsibilities for students, school and parents respectively. This constitutes an inherent paradox in the game because the participants are free to play or not play, since it is only a game, but once they play, they can no longer decide not to play. The game is designed in a way so that it seems optional whether or not one wants to play but turns out to be binding should withdrawal be desired.

The analysis of the political games showed that the definition of boundaries shifts from general decisions to interaction with those involved, where the establishment of boundaries is no longer tied to the organizational premise machine. The creation games provide organizations with the possibility of playing with their boundaries and to put them at stake in multiple interactions. Public institutions can shift the redefinition of own constitutive conditions from political centres of decision to ongoing interactive work with boundaries. Creation games make it possible to put constitutive boundaries at stake while maintaining the boundaries' condition of 'being at stake'. This defines interface interaction as permanent political games. That is, play as fluid power. This shift renders the formation of boundaries particular, fluid and personal. Boundaries become particular in relation to specific systems of interaction and the same applies to their validity. Thus, boundaries become fluid in that they can always continue to be the object of play and they continue at the same time to be both binding and non-binding. Finally, boundaries seem to have been made personal in their character of internal dedication from those involved.

When boundaries become defined as tied to creation games through interaction, strategy becomes immanent in the games. The creation games constitute a strategic possibility to define the way in which systems in the environment create themselves and make themselves relevant to their environment in specific ways. The creation games unite strategy and play in an ongoing challenge to create an environment that makes itself relevant and valid.

Even when someone's intentions are very different from play, and even when someone is selected last of all, they are still part of the game, and the nature of play is such that it is able to integrate multiplicity under the aegis of unity and allow this encounter to exist in the game and on the game's own terms. No answer is required – only the continuation of the game.

This leads to a question concerning play, power and pedagogy in creation games. I analysed pedagogy as a communicative code that divides the world into better and worse in terms of learning. Pedagogical communication seeks to control socialization, but socialization remains the untouchable outside of pedagogy. Likewise, I analysed power as a communicative code that divides the world into power-inferiority and power-superiority. Power communication seeks to operate as the ultimate form of coercion, but freedom of action remains the untouchable outside of power. I then analysed the ways in which play and games evoke couplings between play, power and pedagogy in the different semantic periods. I concluded that competition games imply that power communication is able to parasite on play as form without permitting play to unfold its own form. The training and simulation games, on the other hand, imply that pedagogical communication parasites on play as form. Thus, play becomes subordinated to the pedagogical perspective with a view to learning. The training games suggest a loose coupling between power and pedagogy where power can observe pedagogy as the disciplining of roles, and where pedagogy sees power as learning objective. In the social creation games, play is recognized for its own logic in both power communication and pedagogical communication. Power as form is doubled in power and empowerment, and it is in the empowerment

Time	Play as form	The relation play/power/pedagogy
From 1860	Competition games	Power parasites on the code of play
From 1955	Training and simulation games	Power and pedagogy are coupled and pedagogy parasites on the code of play
From 1980	Social creation games	Play and pedagogy are coupled in empowerment as the doubled form of power

Figure C.1　The coupling over time of play, power, and pedagogy

framing that play, power and pedagogy are coupled. That results in a peculiar form of power, which suspends itself only in order to re-emerge in a new form. The creation games as form plays power and its conditions into existence, including the very distinction between the power-superior and the power-inferior. This can be summed up diagrammatically as shown in Figure C.1.

Altogether, I have conducted a contemporary diagnosis of the emergence and dislocation of organizational games and have shown that the games, which currently turn up everywhere in political organizations, private companies, and voluntary organizations, represent more than an arbitrary trend. Creation games represent a response to the challenges in modern organizations associated with managing integration in the context of immense pressures to adapt. We are not about to see creation games disappear because these games have assumed a function that cannot easily be substituted by alternative forms. The pressure to adapt makes it necessary for organizations to allow a much greater communicative differentiation, including a much greater level of situational complexity management, where the premises for such management are deferred to the management itself. That undermines the organization's function as premise machine. It results in a self-deconstructive organization, working with premises, which are partially deferred and partially oscillating between being both binding (decisions) and non-binding (play). Through play, the organization is able to perform risk management in relation to its continual process to sustain alternatives and temporarily bracket the organization's own premises. Through play, the organization is able to manage its own contingency and hence the possibility of always being much more than itself. Play in organization began with the emergence of particular forms that were recognizable by their symbols as play. However, the central question is whether play continues to be tied to specific forms or whether play has also been raised to a general medium through which the organization is able to observe itself and thereby designate certain activities and decisions as play regardless of their symbolic manifestations. This would turn play into a general machine for risk management.

However, as we have seen, creation games also put many things at stake. Organizing games for employees, parents, teams, and others is more than a game. Each of the creation games put a certain nexus of play, power and pedagogy at stake, and this should be kept in mind by both organizers and players of these games:

- If I, as the principal, decide to have my teachers engage in games with parents at parent meetings, what is the form of power I exercise? What type of power do I relinquish? What are the communicative spaces that I encourage the creation of, and what roles are assigned in these spaces for parents, teachers and students respectively? Which new relationships do I allow for between school and family? What options do I grant the participants in terms of choosing to either play or not play? Which (im)possibilities do I create for not playing? What types of commitment do I put on the participants? What status should be granted the results of the games? And how do we move on after the game? Should the game be played continually?
- If I tell the children to play 'Short and sweet', does it turn into a game for the children? Does it develop into more than a game? Does it lead to communication about the hierarchy among the children on the pretext of play? When a teacher asks a child to make a statement about another child, is it fair to expect that the child is aware of how it becomes visible in the communication? When engaging in play-conversation in order to learn to articulate and create transparency, what other issues are then rendered invisible?

- In 'Health at play', a game is suddenly transformed into a collective agreement. It is a double bound communication. If I as manager instruct citizens or employees to play a game, is the game then double bound? Have I organized the game in a way so that it is simultaneously non-binding and binding? How does it affects the game rules of the communication if it is double bound, and what are the risks involved for the individual player as well as for the communication's possibilities for development?

- If as a leader, I want to create a workplace with a good atmosphere, fortitude, and humour by organizing fun competitions and events, how do I make sure that these do not become the object of ridicule either by employees, managers or the workplace as such?

- If as a manager I organize diversity games in order to increase employees' ability to identify and recognize various sides of each other, how does this affect the possibility of articulating differences such as gender, age and ethnicity as problematic differences in day-to-day interactions?

- If, as a leader of a voluntary organization, I organize dialogue and reflection games for the volunteers in order to avoid constricting rules, do I thereby support or undermine the volunteers' involvement in the organization? Do the volunteers respond positively to reflection and talk? Or have they precisely chosen to become volunteers because they want to make a contribution and *work* as volunteers rather than talk about doing so?

- If, as a leader, classroom teacher, social worker or something else, I organize therapeutic games in order to enable employees, students or citizens to develop and actualize their personality, how is the boundary defined between play, power and therapy? How should it be defined? Is the boundary the same from the respective perspectives of organizer and player of the game? Even if, as a leader, I make it clear that these games are merely an offer and that they should be treated as play, how do I handle the possibility that they might still be observed as power and may result in psychotic language games that undermine employees and citizens despite the intention to achieve the opposite goal? And how do I deal with the fact that I might not be able to observe, not to mention regulate, what takes place in the communication, which I have initiated but which takes on a life of its own once it has begun? How do I make sure that it is always possible for the participants to decide to leave the game and that this possibility is not just theoretical and is without any consequence for those who decide to leave the game? And how do I relate to the possibility that even while striving towards the empowerment of the individual, I might appropriate the very language of freedom and will?

• And finally: what do I do if the game is a complete success and both creation games and other organizational activities are viewed precisely as play and nothing else?

Clearly, these insights need further elaboration in future studies. It seems obvious, for example, to initiate interaction studies of the unfolding of specific games and to explore participant strategies in the games. Do they embrace the game? Do they resist the game? Do they play with the fact that they are playing? Another possibility would be to analyse specific policy fields such as the school system to see how creation games operate in combination with other self- and power technologies. With this book, I have merely tried to put the ball in play.

Bibliography

Aarhus Municipality School Agency (Århus Kommunale Skolevæsen) (2003): *Sammen kan vi mere*. Kroghs Forlag, 2.19–2.23.

Abramis, David (1989): "Finding the fun at work", in *Psychology Today*, March, pp. 36–38.

Ackoff, Russel L. (1959): "Games, decisions, and organizations" in Ludwig von Bertalanffy & Anatol Rapoport (eds.): *General Systems, Yearbook of Society for General Systems*, vol. IV, Michigan.

Æsopromanen (2003): *anonym forfatter*. Museum Tusculanums Forlag, København.

Ahamer, Gilbert (2004): "Negotiate your future: Web-based role play", *Campus-Wide Information Systems*, vol. 21, no. 1, pp. 35–58.

Andersen, Niels Åkerstrøm (1995): *Selvskabt forvaltning*. Nyt fra Samfundsvidenskaberne, København.

Andersen, Niels Åkerstrøm (1996): *Udlicitering - Når det private bliver politisk*. Nyt fra Samfundsvidenskaberne, København.

Andersen, Niels Åkerstrøm (1997): *Udlicitering – Strategi og historie*. Nyt fra Samfundsvidenskaberne, København.

Andersen, Niels Åkerstrøm (2002): "Polyfone organisationer", *Nordiske OrganisationsStudier*, no. 2, pp. 27–53.

Andersen, Niels Åkerstrøm (2003): *Borgerens kontraktliggørelse*. Hans Reitzels Forlag, København.

Andersen, Niels Åkerstrøm (2004a): "Ledelse af personlighed – om medarbejderens pædagogisering", in Dorthe Pedersen (ed.): *Offentlig ledelse i managementstaten*. Forlaget Samfundslitteratur, København.

Andersen, Niels Åkerstrøm (2004b): "The contractualisation of the citizen – on the transformation of obligation into freedom", in *Social Systems*, vol. 10, no. 2, pp. 273–291.

Andersen, Niels Åkerstrøm (2005): "Den selv-barnliggjorte voksne" in Carsten Nejst Jensen (ed.): *Voksnes læringsrum*. Billesøe & Baltzer, Værløse.

Andersen, Niels Åkerstrøm, (2007a): "Creating the client who can create himself and his own fate – the tragedy of the citizens' contract" in *Qualitative Sociology Review*, vol. III, no. 2, pp. 119–143. Available online: http://www.qualitativesociologyreview.org/ENG/Volume7/QSR_3_2_Andersen. pdf

Andersen, Niels Åkerstrøm (2007b) "The self-infantilised adult and the management of personality", *Critical Discourse Studies*, vol. 4, no. 3, pp. 331–352.

Andersen, Niels Åkerstrøm (2008a): *Partnerships: Machines of Possibility*. Policy Press, Bristol.

Andersen, Niels Åkerstrøm (2008b) "The World as Will and Adaptation: The inter-discursive coupling of citizens' contracts", *Critical Discourse Studies*, vol. 5, no. 1, pp. 75–89.

Andersen, Niels Åkerstrøm & Asmund Born (2000): "Complexity and change: Two 'semantic tricks' in the triumphant oscillating organization", *System Practice and Action Research*, vol. 13, no. 3, pp. 297–328.

Andersen, Niels Åkerstrøm & Asmund Born (2001): *Kærlighed og omstilling*. Nyt fra Samfundsvidenskaberne, København.

Andersen, Niels Åkerstrøm & Asmund Born (2005): "Selvet mellem undersøgelse og bekendelse – En inklusions og eksklusionsmaskine", *Grus*, no. 74, pp. 94–114.

Andersen, Niels Åkerstrøm & Asmund Born (2007a): "Heterophony and the postponed organisation – Organizing autopoietic systems", *Tamara Journal for Critical Organizational Inquiry*, vol. 6, no. 6.2, pp. 176–186.

Andersen, Niels Åkerstrøm & Asmund Born (2007b): "Emotional identity feelings as communicative artefacts in organisations", *International Journal of Work Organisation and Emotion*, vol. 2, no. 1, pp. 35–48.

Andersen, Niels Åkerstrøm & Asmund Born (2008): "The Employee in the Sign of Love", *Culture and Organization*, vol. 14, no. 4, pp. 225–343.

Andersen, Niels Åkerstrøm & Niels Thyge Thygesen (2004): "Selvskabelsesteknologier i den selvudsatte organisation", *Grus*, no. 73, pp. 8–29.

Andlinger, G.R. (1958a): "Business games – play one!" in *Harvard Business Review*, Marts/April pp. 115–125.

Andlinger, G.R. (1958b): "Looking around", *Harvard Business Review*, July/August, pp. 147–160.

Ariés, P. (1973): *Centuries of Childhood*. Penguin Books, Harmondsworth.

Association Management (2001): "Playing to stay ahead of the game", July.

Baecker, Dirk (1999): "The form game" in Dirk Baecker (ed.): *Problems of Form*. Stanford University Press, Stanford, CA.

Bateson, Gregory (2000): *Steps to an Ecology of Mind – Collected essays in Anthropology, Psychiatry, Evolution, and Epistemology*. University of Chicago Press, Chicago.

Bille, Steen (2005): "Fodbold løser konflikter", available online: http://www.dgi.dk/nyheder/vis_nyhed.aspx?ID=5997&D=30.

Blekinsopp, John (2007): "The ties that double bind us: Career, emotion and narrative coping in difficult working ralationships", *Culture and Organization*, vol. 13. no. 3, pp. 251–266.

Boje, David, Michaele Driver & Yue Cai (2005): "Fiction and humour in transforming McDonald's narrative strategies", *Culture and Organization*, vol. 11. no. 3, pp. 195–208.

Bok, Edward W. (1925): *Twice Thirty*. Charles Scribner's Sons, New York.

Borch, Christian (2005): *Kriminalitet og magt*. Forlaget politisk revy, København.

Borden, Neil (1925): "The Harvard advertising awards", in *Harvard Business Review*, vol. 3, no. 3, April, pp. 257–264.

Bowman, John R. (1987): "Making work play" in Gary Alan Fine (ed.): *Meaningful Play, Playful Meaning*, Human Kinetics Publisher, Champaign, IL.

Brown, Michael (1990): "The bone game: A ritual of transformation", in *Journal of Experimental Learning*, vol. 13, pt. 1, pp. 48–52.

Cabot, Philip (1925): "Competition is the life of trade", *Harvard Business Review*, vol. 3, no. 4, July, pp. 386–393.

Caillois, Roger (1982): *Die Spiele und die Menschen*. Ullstein Materialien, Berlin.

Campbell, Forrest, Donald Pierce & Paul Torgersen (1964): "The maintenance game", *The Journal of Industrial Engineering*, vol. 15, no. 1, pp. 30–36.

Carlson, John G. H. & Michael J. Misshauk (1972): *Introduction to Gaming: Management Decision Simulations*, John Wiley & Sons, Inc., New York.

Caroselli, Marlene (1996): *Quality Games for Trainers*. The McGraw-Hill Companies, New York.

Centre for Voluntary Social Work (Center for Frivilligt Socialt Arbejde) (2002): *Værdier på spil – et debatspil om menneskesyn og personlige værdier i det frivillige sociale arbejde*. Odense.

Centre for Voluntary Social Work (Center for Frivilligt Socialt Arbejde) (2004): *Frivillig*, vol. 12, no. 72, 1–12.

Centre for Voluntary Social Work (Center for Frivilligt Socialt Arbejde) (2005): *Holdningsspil om frivilligpolitik*, Odense.

Christensen, Gudrun & Niels Åkerstrøm Andersen (1999): "Spisningens sygeliggørelse", *Grus*, no. 59, pp. 23–44.

Christian, William (1961): "Don't bet on business games", *Business Automation*, July, pp. 22–25, 66.

Christopher, Elizabeth M. & Larry E. Smith (1991): *Negotiation Training Through Gaming, Strategies, Tactics and Manoeuvres*. Kogan Page, London/Nichols Publishing, New York.

Clam, Jean (2000): "System's sole constituent: The operation", *Acta Sociologica*, vol. 43, no. 1, pp. 63–80.

Clarke, John & Janet Newman (1997): *The Managerial State*. Sage, London.

Cohen, K. J., R. M. Cyert, W. R. Dill, A. A. Kuehn, M. H. Miller & P. R. Winters (1960): "The Carnegie tech management game", *The Journal of Business*, vol. 33, no. 4, pp. 303–321.

Cohen, K. J., W. R. Dill, A. A. Kuehn & P. R. Winters (1964): *The Carnegie Tech Management Game. An Experiment in Business Education*, Richard D. Irwin, Inc., Homewood, IL.

Copenhagen Municipality (Københavns Kommune) (2002): *Værdifuld ledelse*. CD-Rom udviklet I et samarbejde mellem Zenaria og Københavns Kommune, Økonomiforvaltningen, 5. kontor, Zenaria.

Corsun, David, Cheri Yong & Amy McManus (2006): "Overcoming managers' perceptual shortcuts through improvisational theatre games", *Journal of Management Development*, vol. 25, no. 4, pp. 298–315.

Costea, Bogdan, Norman Crump & John Holm (2005): "Dionysus at work? The ethos of play and the ethos of management", in *Culture & Organization*, vol. 11, no. 2, pp. 139–151.

Costea, Bogdan, Norman Crump & John Holm (2006): "Conceptual history and the interpretation of managerial ideologies", *Management & Organizational History*, vol. 1, no. 2, pp. 159–175.

Cour, Anders la (2003): "Den forlegne organisation", *Grus*, Årg. 24, nr. 70, pp. 62–78.

Cronen, Vernon E., Johnson, Kenneth M., Lannamann, John, W. (1982): "Paradoxes, double binds, and reflexive loops: An alternative theoretical perspective", in *Family Process*, vol. 21, no. 1, pp. 91–112.

Cruikshank, Barbara (1999): *The Will to Empower Democratic Citizens and the Subjects*. Cornell University Press, London.

Cruikshank, Barbara (2004): "Viljen til at mægtiggøre: Medborgerskabsteknologier og 'Krigen mod Fattigdom'", *Grus*, no. 70, pp. 30–48.

Csikszentmihalyi, Mihaly (2000): *Beyond Boredom and Anxiety*, Jossey-Bass Inc. Publishers, San Francisco, CA.

Dahlager, Lisa (2005): "I samtalens rum – en magtanalyse med afsæt i den livsstilsrelaterede forebyggelsessamtale", PhD dissertation, Institut for Folkesundhedsvidenskab, Københavns Universitet.

Danish Road safety Council (Rådet for Større Færdselssikkerhed) (2006a): *Cykelspurten*. Et brætspil, (det præcise årstal er ukendt), København.

Danish Road safety Council (Rådet for Større Færdselssikkerhed) (2006b): *Kasper og split får nye cykler*. Et vendespil, København.

Danish Veterinary and Food Administration (Fødevarestyrelsen), National Board of Health (Sundhedsstyrelsen) and School and Society (Skole og Samfund) (2007): *Sundhed på spil – dialog og samarbejde om klassens sundhed*. Et spil, København.

Dean, Mitchell (2007): *Governing Societies*. Open University Press, Maidenhead, UK.

Dickinson, Clarck (1937): *Compensating Industrial Effort*. Macdonald & Evans, London.

Dodgson, Mark, Gann, David & Salter, Ammon (2005): *Think, play, do*. Oxford University Press, Oxford.

Dreier, Horst (1991): *Hierarchische Verwaltung in demokratischen Staat*. J.C.B Mohr (Poul Siebeck), Tübingen.

Eifermann, Rivka (1970): "Cooperativeness and egalitarianism in Kibbutz children's games", *Human Relations*, vol. 32, no. 6, pp. 579–587.

Elgood, C. (1996): *Using Management Games*. Gower Press, Aldershot.

Fleming, Peter (2005): "Workers' playtime: Boundaries and cynicism in a 'culture of fun' programme" *Journal of Applied Behavioural Science*, vol. 41, no. 3, pp. 285–303.

Foerster, Heinz von (1989): "Warhnemung", in J. Baudrillard, H. Börhringer, V. Flusser, H.V. Foerster, K. Friedrich & P. Weibel (eds.): *Philosophien der neuen Technologie*, Merve Verlag, Berlin, pp. 27–41.

Foerster, Heinz von (1992) "Ethics and second-order cybernetics", in *Cybernetics & Human Knowing*, vol. 1, no. 1, pp. 9–19.

Forbess-Greene, Sue (1983): *The Encyclopedia of Icebreakers*. Applied Skills Press, San Diego.

Foucault, Michel (1977): *Discipline and Punish*. Penguin, London.

Foucault, Michel (1986): *The Archaeology of Knowledge*. Tavistock Publications, London.

Foucault, Michel (1988): "The ethic of care for the self as a practice of freedom", in James Bernauer & David Rasmussen (eds.): *The Final Foucault*, The MIT Press, Cambridge, MA.

Gadamer, Hans-Georg (1985): *Truth and Method*. Crossroad, New York.
Gardner, Howard (1997): *De mange intelligensers pædagogik*. Gyldendal, København.
Gauntlett, David (2006): "David Guntlett on LEGO Serious Play", available online: http://www.artlab.org.uk/lego.htm
Gauntlett, David (2007): *Creative Explorations*. Routledge, New York.
Graham, Robert G. & Clifford F. Gray (eds.) (1969): *Business Games Handbook*. American Management Association, Inc., OR.
Greene, Jay R. & Roger L. Sisson (1959): *Dynamic Management Decision Games*. John Wiley & Sons, London.
Greenlaw, Paul S. & Stanford S. Kight (1960): "The human factor in business games", *Business Horizons*, vol. 3, no. 3, pp. 55–61.
Greenwich, Carolyn (1997): *The Fun Factor*. The McGraw-Hill Companies, Australia.
Greenwich, Carolyn (2000): *Fun and Gains. Motivate and Energize Staff with Workplace Games, Contest and Activities*. McGraw Hill, Australia.
Groos, Karl (1976): *The Play of Man*. Arno Press, New York.
Hall, Anthony S. & Jimmy Algie (1974): A *Management Game for the Social Services*. Bedford Square Press, London.
Hansen, Carl Olav (1997a): *Ærligt snak - I, Et samtalespil til forældremøde fra Børnehaveklasse – 5. klasse*, (det præcise årstal er ukendt), Special-Pædagogisk Forlag, Herning.
Hansen, Carl Olav (1997b): *Gult kort til Ebbe, en film om "Kort og godt"*. (det præcise årstal er ukendt), Special-Pædagogisk Forlag, Herning.
Hansen, Carl Olav (1997c): *Kort og godt i familien*. (det præcise årstal er ukendt), Special-Pædagogisk Forlag, Herning.
Hansen, Carl Olav (1997d): *Kort og godt i indskolingen*. (det præcise årstal er ukendt), Special-Pædagogisk Forlag, Herning.
Hansen, Carl Olav (1997e): *Kort og godt. Et socialpædagogisk spil. Grønt spil: 3.-6. klasse. Blåt spil: 7.-10. klasse*. (det præcise årstal er ukendt), Special-Pædagogisk Forlag, Herning.
Harvard Business Review (1924a): "Incentive systems of wage payment", vol. 2, no. 4, July, pp. 474–480.
Harvard Business Review (1924b): "The use of contest among salesmen", vol. 2, no. 4, July, pp. 480–489.
Hickman, Craig R. (1995): *The Productivity Game*. Prentice Hall, New Jersey.
Hjort, Daniel (2004): "Creating space for play/invention – concepts of space and organizational entrepreneurship", in *Entrepreneurship & Regional Development*, 16, September, pp. 413–432.
Hohmann, Luke (2007): *Innovation games. Creating breakthrough products through collaborative play*. Addison-Wesley, London.
Huizinga, Johan (1936) [1971]: *Homo Ludens*. Beacon Press.
Hutte, Herman (1965): "Decision-taking in a management game", *Human Relations*, no. 1, pp. 5–20.
Hydle, Ida (2003): "Regering af helse: Fra pasient til risikant", in Iver B. Neumann & Ole J. Sending (eds.): *Regjering i Norge*, Pax Forlag, Oslo.

Højlund, Holger & Anders la Cour (2008): "Voluntary social work as paradox", *Acta Sociologica*, vol. 51, no. 1, pp. 929–938.

Højlund, Holger & Lars Thorup Larsen (2001): "Det sunde fællesskab", *Distinktion*, nr. 3, pp. 73–90.

Illustreret Tidende (1861): "Fra Landmandsforsamlingen i Horsens", *Årgang nr.* 2, nor. 98, 11/8–1861, s. 346, 370.

Illustreret Tidende (1862): "Danmark på verdensudstillingen i London 1862", *Årgang nr.* 3, nr. 147, 20/7–1862, s. 342.

Illustreret Tidende (1872): "Industriuddelingens Præmieuddeling", *Årgang nr.* 13, nr. 677, 15/9–1872, s. 468, 470.

Janner, Richard (1971): *50 års firmaidræt.* Firma-klubbernes Boldspil Union, København.

Jessop, Bob (1999): "The dynamics of partnership and governance failure", in G. Stoker (ed.) *The New Politics of Local Governance in Britain.* Oxford University Press, Oxford.

Jones, Alanna (1996): *The Wrecking Yard of Games and Activities.* Idyll Arbor, Inc., Ravensdale, WA.

Jones, Alanna (1998): *104 Activities that Build.* Rec Room Publishing, Richland, WA.

Jones, Ken (1989): *A Sourcebook of Management Simulations.* Nichols Publishing, New York.

Jones, Ken (1994): *Icebreakers – A Sourcebook of Games, Exercises and Simulations.* Kogan Page, London.

Kaagan, Stephen S. (1999): *Leadership Games.* Sage Publication, Thousand Oaks, CA.

Knudsen, Hanne (2007): "Familieklassen – nye grænser mellem skole og hjem", in Lejf Moos (ed.): *Nye sociale teknologier i folkeskolen – kampen om dannelsen.* Dafolo Forlag, Frederikshavn.

Knudsen, Hanne (2008): "Forældreledelse. Let's be careful out there!" in Camilla Sløk & Kaspar Villadsen (eds.): *Velfærdsledelse – Ledelse og styring i den selvledende velfærdsstat.* Hans Reitzels Forlag, København.

Knudsen, Morten (2005): "Displacing the paradox of decision making – the management of contingency in the modernization of a Danish county", in David Seidl and Kai Helge Becker (eds.) (2005): *Niklas Luhmann and Organization Studies.* Liber and CBS press, Fredriksberg, Denmark.

Knudsen, Morten (2006): "Autolysis Within Organizations – A Case Study", *Soziale Systeme* vol. 12, no. 1, pp. 79–99

Kociatkiewicz, Jerzy (2000): "Dreams of time, times of dreams: Stories of creation from roleplaying game sessions", *Studies in Culture, Organization, and Society*, vol. 6, pp. 71–86.

Kroehnert, Gary (2001): *103 Additional Training Games.* McGraw Hill, Australia.

Lansburgh, Richard & William Spriegel (1940): *Industrial Management.* John Wiley & Sons, Inc., London.

Lowood, Henry (2006): "Game studies now, history of science then", *Games and Culture*, vol. 1, no. 1, pp. 68–71.

Luhmann, Niklas (1979): *Trust and Power*, John Wiley & Sons, Chichester.

Luhmann, Niklas (1985): *A Sociological Theory of Law*. Routledge & Kegan Paul: London.

Luhmann, Niklas (1989): *Ecological Communication*. The University of Chicago Press, Chicago.

Luhmann, Niklas (1990): *Political Theory in the Welfare State*. Walter de Gruyter: Berlin/New York.

Luhmann, Niklas (1992): "Operational closure and structural coupling" in *Cardozo Law Review*, vol. 13, no. 5, pp. 1419–1441.

Luhmann, Niklas (1993a) "Die Paradoxie des Entscheidens", in *Verwaltungs-Archiv. Zeitschrift für Verwaltungslehre, Verwaltungsrecht und Verwaltungspolitik*, vol. 84, no. 3, pp. 287–299.

Luhmann, Niklas (1993b): "Barnet som medium for opdragelse", in Cederstrøm, Qvortrup og Rasmussen (eds.): *Læring, Samtale, Organisation – Luhmann og Skolen*. Unge pædagoger, København, pp. 160—190.

Luhmann, Niklas (1993c): *Gesellschaftsstruktur und Semantik, Band 1*. Suhrkamp, Frankfurt am Main, pp. 9–72.

Luhmann, Niklas (1993d): "Deconstruction as second-order observing", in *New Literary History*, vol. 24, pp. 763–782.

Luhmann, Niklas, (1995): *Social Systems*. Stanford University Press, Stanford.

Luhmann, Niklas (1996): "Membership and motives in social system", *Systems Research*, vol. 13, no. 3, pp. 341–348.

Luhmann, Niklas (1999): "The paradox of form", in D. Backer (ed.): *Problems of Form*. Stanford University Press, Stanford.

Luhmann, Niklas (2000) *Organisation und Entscheidung*. Westdeutscher Verlag, Wiesbaden.

McAteer, Peter (1991): "Simulations: learning tools for the 1990s", *Training & Development*, vol. 45, no. 10, pp. 19–26.

McGillivray, David (2005): "Fitter, happier, more productive: Governing working bodies through wellness", *Culture and Organization*, vol. 11. no. 2, pp. 125–138.

Mainemelis, Charalampos & Sarah Ronson (2006): "Ideas are born in fields of play: Towards a theory of play and creativity in organizational settings", *Research in Organisational Behaviour: An Annual Series of Analytical Essays and Critical Reviews Research in Organizational Behaviour*, vol. 27, pp. 81–131.

Maller, Julius Bernard (1929): *Cooperation and Competition*. Bureau of Publications, New York.

March, James G. and Johan P. Olsen (1976): *Ambiguity and Choice in Organizations*. University Press of Norway, Bergen.

March, James G. (1981): "Footnotes to organizational change", *Administrative Science Quarterly*, vol. 26, pp. 563–577.

March, James G. & Barbara Levitt (1988): "Organizational learning", *Annual Review of Sociology*, vol. 14, 319–340.

Marshall, S. L. A. (1947): *Men Against Fire*. William Morrow & Company, New York.

Marx, Karl (1964): *Selected Writing in Sociology and Social Philosophy*. McGraw-Hill, New York.

Mead, Georg Herbert (2005): *Sindet, selvet og samfundet*. Akademisk Forlag, København.

Miller, Jacqueline (1996): "Humour – an empowerment tool for 1990s", *Empowerment in Organizations*, vol. 4, no. 2, pp. 16–21.

Miller, Jacqueline (1997): "All work and no play may be harming your business", in *Management Development Review*, vol. 10, no. 6/7, pp. 254–255.

Ministry of Health (Sundhedsministeriet) (1999): *Regeringens Folkesundhedsprogram 1999–2008*, København.

Ministry of Interior and Health (Indenrigs- og Sundhedsministeriet) (2006): *Idekatalog til folkesundshedsprogram*, EM 2006/39, Jr. 45.47.15.

Mintzberg, Henry (1993): *Structures in five: Designing effective organizations*, Englewoods Cliffs, N.J.: Prentice Hall.

Münch, Richard (1992): "Autopoiesis by definition", *Cardozo Law Review*, vol. 13, no. 5, pp. 1463–1471.

Nanus, Burt (1969): "Management games: An answer to critics", in Robert G. Graham & Clifford F.Gray (eds.): *Business Games Handbook*. American Management Association, Inc., New York.

National Board of Health (Sundhedsstyrelsen) (1999): "Føl dig frem – et debatmateriale om kærlighed, lyster og følelser", Rapport udarbejdet af Mette Kort, Camilla Munch, Michael Krag og Michael Jørgensen for Sundhedsstyrelsen, April.

National Council on Public Health (Det Nationale Råd for Folkesundhed) (2002): *10 gode grunde til IKKE at forebygge!*, København.

Newman, Janet (2001): *Modernising Governance*. Sage, London.

Newstrom, John W. & Edward E. Scannell (1980): *Games Trainers Play. Experiential Learning Exercises*. McGraw Hill Book Company, New York.

Newstrom, John & Edward E. Scannell (1998): *The Big Book of Team Building Games*. McGraw-Hill, New York.

Nielsen, Klaus (2005): "Frelserpædagogik og selvrealisering – moderne bekendelsesformer i dansk pædagogik", in Svend Brinkmand & Cecilie Eriksen (eds.): *Selvrealisering – Kritiske diskussioner af en grænseløs udviklingskultur*, Klim, Århus.

Philippopoulos-Mihalopoulos, Andreas (2003): "Suspension of suspension", *Law and literature*, vol. 15, no. 3, pp. 345–370.

Pike, Bob & Lynn Solem (2000): *50 Creative Training Openers & Energizers*. Jossey-Bass/Pfeiffer & Creative Training Techniques Press, San Francisco, CA.

Pottage, A. (1998): "Power as an art of contingency: Luhmann, Deleuze, Foucault", *Economy & Society*, vol. 27, no. 1, pp. 1–27.

Regional Networks for Companies' Social Involvement (De regionale netværk for virksomhedernes sociale engagement) (2005): *Ansvar på tværs. Et spil*, Zentropa Interaction Aps.

Rennison, Bettina (2007a): "Historical Discourses of Public Management in Denmark", *Management & Organizational History*, vol. 2, no. 1, pp. 5–26.

Rennison, Bettina (2007b): "Cash, Codes and Complexity: New adventures in the public management of pay scales", *Scandinavian Journal of Management*, vol. 23, no. 2, pp. 146–167.

Right to Play (2007a): "How to play a *right to play* game", available online: http://www.righttoplay.com/site/PageServer?pagename=game_ infection_protection

Right to Play (2007b): "Our programme", available online: http://www.rightto play.com/site/PageServer?pagename=ourprograms

Right to Play (2007c) "Physical infrastructure development" available online: http://www.righttoplay.com/site/PageServer?pagename=modules

Robertson, Robin (1999): "Some-thing from no-thing: G. Spencer-Brown's Laws of form", *Cybernetics & Human Knowing*, vol. 6, no. 4, pp. 43–55.

Romero, Eric (2005): "The effect of humour on mental state and work effort", *International Journal of Work Organisation and Emotion*, vol. 1, no. 2, pp. 137–149.

Roth, Walter (1976): *Games, Sports and Amusement*. Arno Press, New York.

Sand, Inger-Johanne (1996): *Styring av kompleksitet*. Fakbokforlaget, Bergen-Sandviken.

Scannell, Edward, John Newstrom & Carolyn Nilson (1998): *The Complete Games Trainers Play: Volume II*. The McGraw-Hill Companies, New York.

Schrage, Michael (2000): *Serious Play*. Harvard Business School Press, Boston, MA.

Scott, Walter, Robert Clothier, S.B. Mathewson & William Spriegel (1941): *Personnel Management*. McGraw-Hill Book Company, London.

Semey, Mette (2004): *Digitale rollespil i produktionshallen. En analyse af læringspotentialet i samspillet mellem medie og kommunikation*, PhD dissertation, Center for Industriel Produktion, Institut for Produktion, Aalborg Universitet.

Shubik, Martin (1975): *Games for Society, Business and War*. Elsevier, New York.

Smith, A., T. B. Scobel & R. J. le Frois (1969): "General Motors Institute experiences with business gaming", in Robert G. Graham. & Clifford F. Gray (eds.): *Business Games Handbook*, American Management Association, Inc., New York.

Sommer, Albrecht (1932): "Premium advertising", *Harvard Business Review*, vol. 10, no. 2, January, pp. 203–210.

Spencer-Brown, George (1969): *Laws of Form*. George Allen and Unwin, London.

Steinkuehler, Constance (2006): "Why game (culture) studies now?", *Games and Culture*, vol. 1, no. 1, pp. 97–102.

Stewart, William (1996): "ISO 9000 work instruction – subject: fun", *The TQM Magazine*, vol. 8, no. 4, pp. 17–19.

Sugar, Steve & George Takacs (2000): *Games that Teach Teams*. Jossey-Bass/Pfeiffer, San Francisco, CA.

Sun, Hongyi (1998): "A game for the education and training of production/ operation management", *Education and Training*, vol. 40, no. 9, pp. 411–416.

Sørensen, Jan K. (1980): "Firmaidræt i Danmark", in *Den Jyske Historiker*, nr. 19–20, s. 204–223.

Teubner, Gunther (1991): "Autopoiesis and steering: how politics profit from the normative surplus of capital", in R. Veld, L. Schaap, C. Termeer & M. Twist (eds.): *Autopoiesis and Configuration Theory: New Approaches to Social Steering*, Kluwer Academic Publisher, London.

Thiagarajan, Sivasailam (2006). *Thiagi's 100 Favorite Games*. John Wiley & Sons, Inc., San Francisco, CA.

Thygesen, Niels Thyge & Niels Åkerstrøm Andersen (2007): "The polyphonic effects of technological changes in public sector organization: A system theoretical approach", *Ephemera*, vol. 7, no. 2, 326–345.

Turner, David (1996): *60 Role Plays for Management and Supervisory Training*. The McGraw-Hill Companies, New York.

Virtual Leader Business Skills Suit, available online: http://www.simulearn.net/ leadershiptraining/leadership_simulations.html

Wind, H. C. (1987): *Historie og forståelse*. Aarhus Universitetsforlag, Århus.

Yee, Nick (2006): "The labour of fun. How video games blur the boundaries of work and play",*Games and Culture*, vol. 1, no. 1, pp. 68–71.

Index